I am so excited about *Hope Reborn*! I enjoyed reading it, and Northwood Church will definitely use it. I know of no other resource like it. It takes a person all the way from pre-conversion to being filled with the boldness that comes from the Holy Spirit. Many discipleship materials make too many assumptions that are no longer true in the 21st century. *Hope Reborn* assumes nothing, and presents the Bible's message in a fresh, engaging, and understandable way. I predict this is going to be a very significant resource for the global church.

Bob Roberts Jr.

Founder and Pastor, Northwood Church, Keller, Texas

This book is a great resource to hand to a non-Christian or a new Christian to learn about Jesus Christ and the essentials of Christianity. It is readable, biblical, practical, and helpful. This is a book to buy multiple copies of and have around to give away to people you want to point to Jesus.

Mark Driscoll

Founding Pastor, Mars Hill Church, Seattle, Washington

Tope and Adrian are the real deal – I've preached in their church, fellowshipped with their families, and believe in their ministry. They know and love the Lord and it comes through in *Hope Reborn*. If you are a Christian, this book will help you know and share your faith. And, if you're not, it's a great guide to understand what it means to be a follower of Jesus. I commend them and *Hope Reborn* to you.

Ed Stetzer

President, LifeWay Research, Nashville, Tennessee

An amazing book which will help you follow our amazing Savior.

RT Kendall

Previous minister of Westminster Chapel, London

This book will help newcomers to the faith discover where hope is born and it will help seasoned believers to remember how not to lose it.

Frank Viola
Author of God's Favorite Place on Earth and Jesus Now
frankviola.org, Florida

At last! An engagingly written, theologically vibrant little book that you can give to seekers, to new converts, and to struggling believers. The authors depict a righteous Savior who can be touched and who really cares, and they lay out practical steps every child of God can take to grow strong in the faith.

Michael L. Brown
Author, theologian, apologist, and radio host
lineoffireradio.com Concord, North Carolina

People are often saved through a fragment of truth. What comes next is vital. Here is instruction not only to establish Christians in their new identity but also to provide a path to effective Christian living. Their own burgeoning local church provides a great endorsement to Tope's and Adrian's teaching.

Terry Virgo
Founder of Newfrontiers and well-known Bible Teacher, London

Jubilee Church is an engaging church. They are focussed on the proclamation and demonstration of the gospel, and are growing by conversion. This book will be of great help to anyone who wants to become a Christian. If you have been part of a church for many years *Hope Reborn* will also help you to bring the gospel back to the center, and to become more confident in explaining it to others.

Rice Broocks
Author, God's Not Dead – Evidence for God in an Age of Uncertainty
Nashville, Tennessee

Sometimes I wonder if we see the gospel simply as our door into God's presence instead of regarding the gospel as our only air in God's presence. We don't get over the gospel, but rather we spend a lifetime allowing God to get the gospel into us. This book brilliantly does just that. It simply takes you powerfully into what we all desperately need and never stop needing: Hope. The realest, deepest, truest Hope. If you need some Hope – and, honestly, who doesn't? – I humbly, earnestly recommend these pages to you as real water.

Ann Voskamp
Author of the New York Times Bestsellers, *One Thousand Gifts &*
The Greatest Gift
Ontario, Canada

In every way God's Word measures a man, a husband, father and leader, I have found Tope Koleoso to be authentically gracious, honest, forthright and truthful. He characterizes both Christian love toward all, and mature leadership in The Church. I have spoken in Tope's church a number of times, and readily detect the receptivity and response of a people used to being fed and led in The Word, Its Truth, and into genuine worship and witness as a people. The Body of Christ globally sees the need for a rise of thousands of well-equipped, Christ-like, Holy Spirit empowered, Word-centered and balanced pastors: "this kind" are needed everywhere!

Hope Reborn which Tope has written with one of his leaders will help you grow as a Christian and a leader. Don't make the mistake of thinking this book is for the new Christian only. You will find your love for the gospel growing afresh as you read its pages.

Jack Hayford
Founding Pastor of The Church On The Way
Van Nuys, California

There has long been a need for a short, simple, accessible and biblically faithful book explaining the essence of what it means to be a Christian, how to become a Christian, and how to start living as Christian. *Hope Reborn* meets this need wonderfully. Tope Koleoso and Adrian Warnock explain clearly and concisely the great news of salvation in Jesus, which brings forgiveness, transformation and true hope into our lives. Biblical exposition is combined with pastoral warm, engaging illustrations, real-life stories and practical applications. This book is ideal for those interested in understanding the Christian faith for the first time, for those new to the faith, or for those unsure of their faith. I look forward to using it widely.

John Stevens
National Director, Fellowship of Independent Evangelical Churches
Market Harborough, England

Once, Jesus was teaching and he told people "my burden is light." In other words, he didn't come to weigh us down and make life harder. It seems like there are always people ready to make Christianity complicated and difficult, and that's why I love this book: it captures the simplicity that Jesus originally offered. You need to read this book!

Greg Surratt
Founding pastor of Seacoast Church
Founding board member of the Association of Related Churches (ARC)
Mt. Pleasant, South Carolina

This is an excellent book: simple yet profound, brief yet thorough. Written in a style that is readable and easy to relate to, it covers the critical issues needed for a person to get off to a strong start in their Christian life. I trust and pray that it will be a great resource to many churches and a great blessing to many individuals. May many lives be transformed as a result!

David Smith
Senior Pastor, KingsGate Community Church
Peterborough, England

HOPE
REBORN

HOW TO BECOME A CHRISTIAN
AND LIVE FOR JESUS

Tope Koleoso

and

Adrian Warnock

CHRISTIAN
FOCUS

paperback ISBN 978-1-78191-430-4
epub ISBN 978-1-78191-510-3
Mobi ISBN 978-1-78191-514-1

10 9 8 7 6 5 4 3 2 1

Published in 2014
by
Christian Focus Publications,
Geanies House, Fearn, Ross-shire,
IV20 1TW, Scotland, Great Britain

www.christianfocus.com

Cover design by
Daniel van Straaten

Printed in the U.S.A

CONTENTS

Introduction

We are all either looking for, or glad to have found, hope. Hope brings zest to life. Hope gives strength to face situations that seem overwhelming. Hope helps people leave behind a negative past and capture the purpose for which they were made. Hope renews, it revitalizes, it remakes; it can even make people feel *reborn*.

This book is all about finding the hope which matters above everything else. Millions before you, over thousands of years, have walked this path and found meaning and purpose to life. A life with purpose is a life with vision, and a life with vision has hope. Real hope is found not in a place, or a plan, but in a person: *Jesus Christ* the Son of the Living God.

This short book is designed to help five different types of people.

1. If you are new to Christianity, it focuses on the central message of the Bible, and includes a practical step-by-step guide on how to become a Christian.

2. If you have already explored the faith, our goal in writing is to help you be sure that you are a Christian, and to have a certain hope that you will live forever with Jesus.

3. If you once had a faith in Jesus, but have drifted away from following Him, these pages will help you find your way back to God. He has already taken a step towards you, and is waiting for you to take a step towards *Him*.

4. Or perhaps you have gone to church all your life. Maybe you have always assumed you are a Christian. But many who appear to be Christians will one day hear Jesus say, "I never knew you; depart from me!" (Matthew 7:23). If you think you are already a Christian, you must carefully consider whether or not this really is true (see 2 Corinthians 13:5). This book will help all of us, authors included, with that process.

5. If you are confident that you are a Christian, we hope that these pages will help you to be able to explain what you believe more clearly to others.

We have prayed for you, that Jesus Himself will meet with you as you read this book.

1

The Pharisee and the Prostitute

A popular old Indian hymn, which has also been adapted and set to modern music, declares:

> I have decided to follow Jesus
> No turning back, no turning back.
> The cross before me, the world behind me
> No turning back, no turning back.

These words were originally spoken by the first Christian from a remote village in India. They were his reply when he was asked to deny his faith or else be executed with his whole family. His heartfelt conviction impressed his murderers so much that, despite carrying out their threat, they later converted, along with the whole village.

We hope that by the time you finish reading this book you also will be able to truthfully sing those words, if you can't already.

But before we explore what it means to follow Jesus Christ, we must begin by taking a closer look at who He is.

Why is it that so many people all over the world worship Him 2000 years after He was executed by crucifixion?

Jesus Christ was a carpenter from a rural village who claimed to be the Son of God. Christianity, which takes its name from Him, grew faster and remains larger than any other religion. Today 2.2 billion people describe themselves as Christians.

Let's just say that if Jesus were on Twitter, He would have a lot of followers!

Many people have all kinds of wrong ideas about Jesus. Some think that they cannot come to Jesus because they have said or done things that they know are wrong. They wonder, "How does Jesus feel about me, knowing what I have done?"

> JESUS CHRIST
> Lived 2000 years ago and was executed by crucifixion. He was a carpenter from a rural village, yet Christianity grew faster than any other religion and today 2.2 billion people claim to follow Jesus.

Most of us have a secret sense of guilt, and a fear of being "found out." Perhaps it is things we have done that we regret; actions we have carried out that have wounded other people; or decisions we have made that haunt us.

Other people like to think of themselves as respectable and essentially perfect. They think they are too good to need Jesus.

The truth is most of us think of ourselves in both of these ways at different times. No one is perfect; we are all in the same situation.

Later in this chapter we are going to look at an encounter in the Bible that shows how Jesus sees both these kinds of people.

Many outwardly successful people hide their quiet desperation. They feel inadequate, living without any real hope, joy, peace, or purpose. Some people feel like they are a total failure. Millions of people have found that Jesus is the answer to these feelings and restores our hope.

God is righteous and holy, which means He is perfect and completely separate from all wrongdoing. This causes a barrier between God and humanity. However, despite our actions and attitudes, God continues to love us, and is ready to accept and forgive us. This can be difficult for some people to grasp.

One example of someone who couldn't believe this was a young woman who we will call Amy. She came with her friend to visit me (Tope) when I had recently become a pastor.

Amy was a neatly dressed, beautiful lady, but her face betrayed a hint of fear and low self-confidence. As she spoke, it seemed to me that she knew a lot about God, but didn't have a relationship with him. Amy had something she wanted to talk about, but was afraid.

> ### BORN AGAIN
> When someone who is far from God and therefore spiritually dead, becomes a child of God and is forgiven by Him. They are made new and become spiritually alive to God.

I looked directly at her, encouraging her, "You are in a safe place and will not be judged. If you have done something wrong, God can forgive anything."

Amy began to tell me her story. She described a previous sexual experience that had left her feeling plagued by severe guilt. She went on to say, "I know that God can't forgive me for that, but ..."

I interrupted her mid-sentence, "But God *can* forgive you." Amy was shocked. It was as if she had never heard

13

such a beautiful and profound truth. "God can forgive you," I repeated, "in fact, God wants to forgive you and wipe the past away forever." Sometimes simple words we may have heard a thousand times suddenly take on a new significance for us, as if our eyes have been opened.

At first Amy silently stared at me. Then her tears began to flow. Each time she attempted to ask me another question she sobbed more.

"Yes," I said, "God forgives people, and He loves us, too." Gratitude and relief, and the joy of her guilt being released prompted Amy's tears. What might have taken months of counseling happened in a few moments when Amy, for the first time, really *believed* the good news.

As she listened, Amy immediately turned away from her wrongdoing and towards Jesus. She prayed, and God forgave her. The woman who walked home that evening was free and grateful. The old had gone, and the new had come. This experience of being made new, which the Bible calls being "born again," is what this book is all about.

Being born again is something God does to turn people who are far from God and spiritually dead into people who are spiritually alive; we are born of God, we become His children and are forgiven by Him (John 1:12-13).

Perhaps you have a desire to "become religious." While that is a noble desire, please don't settle for it alone. Instead, we want to introduce you to the living Jesus so you can get to know Him for yourself. Mere religion is not enough.

Mere religion tells you, "You are a sinner." But true Christianity tells you, "There is a Savior who will love you as you are, but will not leave you as you are."

Mere religion highlights your faults and insists you must try harder. But Jesus offers acceptance if you ask for forgiveness, no matter what you have done.

Mere religion says, "You are dirty." But Jesus says, "I can clean you up."

Mere religion is all about principles. But Jesus is all about people.

Mere religion is all about rules. But Jesus is all about grace.

Mere religion demands you earn God's favor. But Jesus loves you unconditionally.

Mere religion condemns. But Jesus forgives.

Mere religion says, "You are a failure." But Jesus says, "I will give you a new beginning, a new identity, and help you to be victorious over sin."

Mere religion sees all the problems in the world and wants to change it. But Jesus says, "Let me start by changing you."

> Mere religion makes you a slave. But Jesus sets you free.

Mere religion makes you a slave. But Jesus sets you free.

Mere religion is a set of rules and regulations. But true Christianity is a relationship with Jesus Christ who lives inside us and empowers us.

Many religious people will reject those who don't follow their standards. Such people are very much like the Pharisees of Jesus' day, a group of religious leaders who precisely interpreted and obeyed the Jewish law without understanding its real purpose. Pharisees would have nothing to do with anyone they considered unworthy. Even today, similar people often stop others from experiencing a real faith.

Faith is not merely striving to obey God and it is more than simply believing certain things about Him. Faith is a response of the heart to God in trust, submission, and dependence. It involves coming to God empty, acknowledging our helplessness, and relying on Him alone to save us. True faith values and cherishes God above everything else, and means we put His reputation and glory above our own desires. Faith is not always perfect, and it can often be mingled with doubt, but it is a settled decision to direct our hearts towards God.

> ### FAITH
>
> A response of the heart to God in trust, submission, and dependence. It involves coming to God empty, acknowledging our helplessness, and relying on Him alone to save us. True faith values and cherishes God above everything else. Despite any ongoing doubts, faith is a settled decision to direct the heart towards God.

Mere religion is a distorted and weakened version of Christianity. If you inject someone with a vaccine made up of a weakened form of an illness, it prevents them from catching the real sickness. Similarly, being exposed to religion often prevents people from grasping the true message of the Bible. The most religious people are often the biggest hypocrites of all, and many secretly commit the very sins they condemn. They forget that God is the only judge with real integrity.

God does not simply excuse our wrongdoing. The Bible calls this sin, which can be defined as a willful failure to follow God's instructions about how we should live. Sin is missing the mark or standard that was set by God. How close we can get to the target impresses us. However, God says, "But you have all missed!" God's target is perfection.

Sin is stepping beyond the boundaries that our Maker has set for us. Sin can often begin as something small and seemingly insignificant. But sin will suck us in so that we are polluted by it. It becomes a part of us so that making us dirty, and everything we think, say or do is in some way contaminated by it. The Bible calls the distortion and damage that sin inflicts on our very personalities "the flesh" or "the sinful nature." Sin is wallowing in actions that God despises.

Ultimately sin is the result of our hearts turning away from valuing God, our Creator. Instead of worshipping Him, we seek fulfillment in created things. We desire pleasure, and look for ways of finding it. We all have a God-shaped hole in our hearts, whether we know it or not, which can never be truly satisfied without worshipping Him. We end up being constantly dissatisfied and unfulfilled with life. We always want just a little bit more. But in the end, only Christ is enough for us.

There is no such thing as a little sin. Even a small error can destroy. The same is true in many areas of life. For example, when we were writing this book, I (Adrian) bought a new bed. While assembling it, I noticed that because a hole had not been properly drilled, a single bolt, intended to hold the slats still, could not be attached.

SIN

A willful failure to follow God's instructions about how to live. Sin involves missing the mark, stepping beyond the boundaries, and wallowing in actions that God despises. Sin pollutes us so that everything we think, say, or do is in some way contaminated by it.

I contacted the manufacturer, who promised to send replacement parts, but agreed that in the meantime the bed could still be used.

However, one night, as my son was getting ready to sleep, there was a splintering noise and the whole bed collapsed. The slats had moved, and in turn putting another part of the bed under pressure that it was not designed to bear. The entire load-bearing section had failed in a dramatic way, with several other screws ripping through solid wood. The bed was useless, and all because of a single missing bolt.

Similarly, if a boat is moored to the harbor by a single chain, and if just one link of that chain fails, it really doesn't matter how strong the rest of the links are, the boat will drift away from where it is meant to be.

In the same way, just one sin is all that it takes for you to be considered unrighteous by God.

To understand Jesus' view of sin and religion, we will examine an occasion when He met a very religious Pharisee and a woman who many scholars believe was a prostitute. This may seem a strange way to begin a book about becoming a Christian. But a Christian is simply a follower of Jesus. Many people today don't understand what Jesus is like. When people meet Him, incredible and surprising things happen.

Jesus was a friend of sinners without ever becoming contaminated by sin. This encounter reveals He was both kind and accepting, yet also holy (which means both sinless and dedicated to God). The story shows us the way he responded to a Pharisee who thought He had lived an honorable life, and a prostitute who knew she hadn't:

> One of the Pharisees asked him to eat with him, and he went into the Pharisee's house and took his place at the table. And behold, a woman of the city, who was a sinner, when she learned that he was reclining at table in the Pharisee's house, brought an alabaster flask of ointment, and standing behind him at his feet, weeping, she began to wet his feet with her tears and wiped them with the hair of her head and kissed his feet and

anointed them with the ointment. Now when the Pharisee who had invited him saw this, he said to himself, "If this man were a prophet, he would have known who and what sort of woman this is who is touching him, for she is a sinner." And Jesus answering said to him, "Simon, I have something to say to you." And he answered, "Say it, Teacher." (Luke 7:36-40)

These events took place in a very conservative culture. The Pharisee and the prostitute would have been very unlikely to ever meet. Similar classes of people exist today who still tend to avoid each other. Many people are unwilling to speak with those they consider "inferior." Unfortunately, some Christians have the reputation of condemning those they call "sinners." They pretend to be pure by rejecting others. Such religious people do not impress Jesus. He accepts anyone who comes to Him humbly, turning away from their sin. Jesus loves everyone.

Christianity is a message of hope. People have infinite value to God. He loves us like parents love their children. He has specifically chosen to adopt us (Ephesians 1:5). All over the world there are Christians trying to demonstrate this to everybody, whatever their background. They are inspired by how Jesus reacted to the Pharisee and the prostitute.

THE INVITATION

The story begins with an invitation. Simon the Pharisee had heard about Jesus and was intrigued enough to invite Him to his home. Many of the Pharisees were Jesus' enemies. Pharisees knew the law of God and pretended they obeyed it. Jesus once stated that no matter how impressive and clean these "holy men" looked on the outside, on the inside they were filthy and as full of death as a tomb (Matthew 23:27). They were hypocrites.

Jesus, a *truly* holy man, had come to town. He hadn't kept Himself separate from the ordinary people, but was performing miracles among them. The Pharisees, who saw themselves as better than everyone else, were not happy about this. They were harsh towards other people and hostile towards Jesus. Often they questioned Him, not because they wanted to know the answer, but because they wanted to humiliate Him in front of onlookers. They were jealous of His popularity, and feared He would undermine their position.

Jesus accepted Simon's invitation, the table was set, and many people were present because crowds followed Jesus wherever He went. Simon may have been very pleased that he had this popular preacher in his house. He had no idea what was about to happen to spoil his dinner party.

THE INTERRUPTION

Suddenly a woman entered the room and went directly to Jesus, disrupting the meal. She was known as a "woman of the city"—a working prostitute—the kind of woman no one wanted to admit they knew. As she approached Jesus, the special guest at this party, she didn't greet Him in a normal way. Instead, she fell down on her knees and began to weep over His feet, and to kiss them. Then she used her hair as a towel to dry them and anointed Him with perfume. The people there must have thought, "What is a prostitute doing in a Pharisee's house?" Simon himself felt disgusted and questioned whether Jesus could truly be a prophet.

In the middle of this awkward scene, Jesus said to Simon, "I have something to say to you." Similarly, as you read, Jesus has something to say to you too, whether you think of yourself as more like the prostitute, the Pharisee, or somewhere in-between.

Jesus told Simon a parable, which is a story that teaches a message, about two servants: one was forgiven a small amount and the other was forgiven much more.

> "A certain moneylender had two debtors. One owed five hundred denarii and the other fifty. When they could not pay, he cancelled the debt of both. Now which of them will love him more?" Simon answered, "The one, I suppose, for whom he cancelled the larger debt." And he said to him, "You have judged rightly." Then turning toward the woman he said to Simon, "Do you see this woman? I entered your house; you gave me no water for my feet, but she has wet my feet with her tears and wiped them with her hair. You gave me no kiss, but from the time I came in she has not ceased to kiss my feet. You did not anoint my head with oil, but she has anointed my feet with ointment. Therefore I tell you, her sins, which are many, are forgiven—for she loved much. But he who is forgiven little, loves little." And he said to her, "Your sins are forgiven." Then those who were at table with him began to say among themselves, "Who is this, who even forgives sins?" And he said to the woman, "Your faith has saved you; go in peace". (Luke 7:41-50)

GOD KNOWS YOUR THOUGHTS

Jesus knew what Simon was thinking. As Simon listened to Jesus' parable, he must have realized "He *knows* me!" God sees deep within the heart; He sees beyond the external. God knows you too, far better than you know yourself.

Jesus responded to Simon's inward thoughts by asking, "Who do you think loved the most?" You can imagine the tone of his voice as Simon reluctantly admitted that it would be the one who had been forgiven the most.

God knows your thoughts toward Him. Are you wondering like Simon, "What kind of man is Jesus? Is He really the Son of God?" He sees how you view others and how you treat them. The parable revealed Simon's wrong attitudes. Jesus effectively said, "You view yourself, Simon, as better than this woman."

This parable makes a very profound and important point. It is something every one of us needs to hear. We all have a tendency to think the worst-case scenario for other people, and the best-case scenario for ourselves. We say of others "They commit sins," but we say of ourselves, " I had a momentary lapse. I tripped up. I made a mistake. It was just a little thing." Sometimes we blame our upbringing, or things that have happened to us. We minimize our own sins, but maximize the sins of others. We feel like poking other people in the eye and saying, "Sinner!" But God sees *all* our thoughts.

Unfortunately, many people who say they are Christians are more similar to the religious Pharisee than to Jesus. It is easy to despise others who have committed sins that we imagine are much worse than our own. Jesus is not like Simon. He does not reject the prostitute, despite her sin. Jesus honors her, while the Pharisee is shown the error of his words.

On the other hand, some people condemn themselves, thinking they are unforgivable. This wrongly suggests that Jesus' death was not enough to enable forgiveness for their own particular sins.

Jesus accepted all kinds of people who came to him, and was well known as a "friend of sinners" (Matthew 11:19). God will still receive you graciously despite whatever you have done, if you come to Him, turn from your sin, and ask Him for help. Jesus will accept you whoever you are and whatever you've done if you come to Him humbly, ask for forgiveness, and make Him your Lord.

You can never appreciate the gospel until you understand that we are all guilty before God, however many or few sins we have committed. Do you take responsibility for your own sin? Do you blame other people instead?

In Jesus' parable, one of the debtors owed fifty denarii, almost two months' wages (a single denarius was approximately a day's wage). The other owed ten times that. Jesus was effectively saying, "Debt is debt." In the same way, sin is sin. This applies to all of us. We are all natural sinners. It comes easily to us. Sin is what we do.

Both servants owed and neither could pay. They both needed help. They both needed a Savior. Somebody cancelled the debt. The same is true for us today. "All have sinned and fall short of the glory of God" (Romans 3:23). All means all. "None is righteous, no, not one" (Romans 3:10). There are no exceptions.

> ### RIGHTEOUSNESS
>
> The state of being where an individual is perfect and free of all sin. When this position of being not guilty is declared to others, a person is justified. When a person knows they are not righteous, guilt and condemnation tend to be the result.

Righteousness is that state of being where an individual is perfect and free of sin. If your position of righteousness is announced and you are declared "not guilty" to others, that is called justification. Many people spend their lives trying to justify themselves, or make themselves look better than they really are. When we know we are not righteous, guilt and condemnation tend to be the result.

There are different types and degrees of sin, but the nature of sin is the same. Some people sin in an obvious way and, like the prostitute's sin, everyone is aware of it. Other people's sin is internal and we think it's "better" because it's hidden. But Jesus sees everything.

The prostitute was very aware of her sexual sin. The Pharisee's sins were pride and self-righteousness. Committing sin demonstrates that you live for yourself, making pleasure your goal. God does hate sin, but He hates pride most of all. Self-righteousness is so subtle, yet it's a very common and grotesque sin because it replaces God with yourself.

Many religious people think, "I am a good person." But they are the only ones impressed with their self-righteousness. God is not at all impressed with our feeble attempts at being holy; to Him they are repulsive. "All our righteous deeds are like a polluted garment" (Isaiah 64:6), this can be translated "filthy rags."

Our own so-called "righteousness" is not enough to get us into heaven. Even the proudest religious people secretly doubt their own purity. We are all afraid that somebody is going to find us out. Pretending we are better than others is deceiving ourselves. When we realize we are in fact far worse than we ever imagined, we are a massive step closer to the solution.

The fact that we are all sinners doesn't make our situation any better. Sin is in all of us whether we are humble enough to recognize it or not. It is imperative for us to learn how it can be dealt with.

God is the only one who is perfect. He sees through all our hypocrisy and all our mixed motives. He knows that at heart we are all about pleasing ourselves. He sees when we are simply trying to look good compared to others. By God's standards, even the best of us fail to measure up. But God knows we are weak, and has compassion on us.

Essentially there are two types of people who are not Christians. The first includes those who know they are sinners, **the unrighteous.** The prostitute is an example of this. A person in this group is very aware that they are essentially full of sin. They may occasionally do good things, but they do not see themselves as righteous.

When such a person meets Jesus, who is full of righteousness, they feel undone. They know they have nothing to offer Him. They feel He could never accept them. In fact, someone in this position often just gives up and sins more and more as they feel they have no hope of ever reaching Jesus' standards.

The second type includes people who think they are better than others. They are **the self-righteous**. All their good deeds cover up the little sins they have committed, so much so that often they don't admit they have sinned even to themselves. Although he doesn't realize it, Simon the Pharisee is actually the bigger sinner because his self-righteousness is so offensive to God.

When a self-righteous person meets Jesus they are cautiously hopeful that He may accept them. They believe they have done many good things, so surely they will be pleasing to God. They believe they deserve rewards from God. But Jesus is the only One who is truly pure and perfect. He alone is full of real righteousness, and is the only One who is **truly righteous**.

Jesus says to all of us, "You shall be holy, for I am holy" (1 Peter 1:16) and, "unless your righteousness exceeds that of the scribes and Pharisees, you will never enter the kingdom of heaven" (Matthew 5:20).

If you are trying to save yourself by your good works you must realize that, no matter how hard you try, you can never convert your inferior self-righteousness so that it matches Christ's perfect righteousness.

There is only one hope. There is only one solution. Jesus washes away both our sin and our self-righteousness, and takes them on His account like a debt. On the cross Jesus took all our sins upon Himself. His righteousness is so great that our unrighteousness is cancelled.

In place of our sin Jesus gives us His own perfect righteousness. God credits Jesus' righteousness to our account by faith (Romans 4:23-25). This declaration is what the Bible calls "justification." It means we are now right with God.

Our sins died with Jesus. Because He rose again we can become truly righteous, first by the decree of God, and then because the righteousness that He places inside of us begins to work its way out. This lifelong process is what the Bible calls "sanctification."

Sadly many people who attend church don't fully understand this truth. Instead they are working hard to try and deserve God's acceptance by their good behavior. Grace is not grace if you earn it. The power of the gospel is released in us when we simply believe:

> For I am not ashamed of the gospel, for it is the power of God for salvation to everyone who believes, to the Jew first and also to the Greek. For in it the righteousness of God is revealed from faith for faith, as it is written, "The righteous shall live by faith." (Romans 1:16-17)

GOD KNOWS THE STATE OF YOUR HEART

The story of the Pharisee and the prostitute, as short as it is, speaks to the Christian. It urges us to realize that those who are forgiven much will demonstrate extravagant love. The prostitute is the hero. She did not care what anyone would say. She gave everything. Lavish grace prompts lavish devotion. True righteousness includes putting Jesus first and worshipping Him.

When you love deeply, it changes the way you worship. How you serve Jesus indicates how much you value Him. This lady demonstrated deep devotion. Forgiveness should rekindle our affection for the One who saved us. It should remind us to also treat "sinners" with love and not reject them, because we all need forgiveness from God.

Jesus effectively gave the Pharisee a very clear message: "You are not as righteous as this woman who has turned to me. Simon, I came to your home but you did not give me any water for my feet. You invited me, but you didn't welcome me properly. This woman's tears washed my feet, and her hair was the towel you didn't offer. You did not kiss my cheek as is the custom, but she kissed my feet. You wanted people to think you were superior, and so you kept your distance. She showed true love because she knows that I have accepted her. I am not looking for people who have convinced themselves that they are righteous when in reality they are not. I am seeking those who you reject as 'sinners' to offer them a new life" (see also Matthew 9:9-13).

The Pharisee was worried about his status, but Jesus pointed him to the prostitute. The Pharisee was all about himself. He needed to understand that life should be all about Jesus.

What does this passage have to say to the person seeking peace with God? Most people do not openly hate God. Instead they may be curious and still have lots of questions. Perhaps that's where you are right now. Jesus will be gracious to you, and is patient while you search for the answers you seek.

This woman sought Jesus in the right way. She did not come pontificating or posturing before Him. She came from behind, demonstrating a kind of reticence or fear: "Will He accept me?" Jesus understood her feelings, and He turned toward her. It's very likely that she had heard His teachings before, and that this was her public declaration of her desire to follow Him.

Jesus knew everything about the prostitute, but accepted her anyway. He knew that her act of devotion was her way of showing that she trusted His love and forgiveness and was leaving her previous way of life. "Therefore," said Jesus, "her sins, which are many, are forgiven." This is how Jesus forgives – completely. Not partially, but totally.

God says about Christians, "I will remember their sin no more" (Jeremiah 31:34).

The Bible is unique in that, except for Jesus, all its heroes have major flaws and these are openly admitted. Peter denied Jesus when it mattered the most, and yet was restored (Luke 22:54-62, John 21). Noah got drunk and sinned, and yet was honored as a man of faith (Genesis 9:21, Hebrews 11:7). King David committed murder, yet when he repented, he was forgiven, and called a man after God's own heart (2 Samuel 11–12, Acts 13:22). The list could go on and on. The lesson here is that God accepts everyone the way they are, but doesn't leave them the way they are. If God can forgive all these people, and use them for His purposes, then there is hope for all of us.

Jesus wants to meet you right now. It doesn't matter who you are, where you are, or what you have done. Jesus might not speak with words, but perhaps you may feel a welling up of love and acceptance from deep within. You will never find greater security than knowing God's forgiveness. Even if you don't feel anything, the Bible tells us that, just like this woman, all who humbly come to Him, asking for forgiveness, will indeed be forgiven. If it takes a while for your emotions to catch up, don't worry. We are not all as expressive as this prostitute was.

Jesus' parable tells us that if you recognize you are indeed in need of Jesus' help, He will accept you. "God opposes the proud, but gives grace to the humble" (James 4:6).

Despite everything that happened, some people watching were still skeptical, thinking, "Oh indeed! Forgive sin? Who can forgive sin?" Jesus performed amazing miracles and yet they refused to believe. But Jesus ignored them. He concentrated on the prostitute and told her what He has also said to millions of others:

"Your faith has saved you. Go in peace."

QUESTIONS TO CONSIDER:

1. How do you think of yourself? Do you think you are more like the Pharisee or the prostitute?

2. Before reading this chapter, did you think that Jesus would be more accepting of those who consider themselves righteous or those who recognize they are sinners?

KEY BIBLE VERSES:

Luke 7:36-50
John 4:1-34

2

Died for you. Raised for you

In the darkness, the crowd of a thousand people from a remote African village murmured restlessly. No matter how many times I (Tope) pulled the cord, the generator would not start.

I would be unable to play *The Jesus Film* after all. My microphone was also useless without power. For a few moments I was unsure what to do. Then I lifted a flashlight above my head. The people quieted expectantly. Suddenly I was

THE GOSPEL

The good news that lost sinners can be reconciled to God forever through the death and resurrection of Jesus, who is now enthroned as ruler of the universe.

gripped by seeing these people in the darkness, and I felt a surge of confidence that I was carrying a message of spiritual light for them. I opened my Bible to John's Gospel and raised my voice to begin to explain the good news about Jesus, the Light of the world.

The message shared that day had a profound impact. This same gospel continues to change people, and bring hope all around the world today. The message focuses on a person, Jesus the Light of the world.

The gospel is the good news that lost sinners can be reconciled to God forever through the death and resurrection of Jesus, who is now enthroned as ruler of the universe:

> For God so loved the world, that he gave his only Son, that whoever believes in him should not perish but have eternal life. (John 3:16)

The Apostle Peter said of Jesus, "There is salvation in no one else" (Acts 4:12). Jesus Himself echoed this radical claim, "I am the way, and the truth, and the life. No one comes to the Father except through me" (John 14:6). Christians believe that the only way to be saved is to ask Jesus for His help. We cannot sort ourselves out. Jesus offers the way to fix our problem.

This gospel is the only thing that can save you. To be helped by this message, you must believe it. Ask God to show you whether it is true.

WHY DO WE NEED TO BE SAVED?

Try not to be alarmed by some of the unfamiliar words in the following verse. We will explain them all.

> All have sinned and fall short of the glory of God, and are justified by his grace as a gift, through the redemption that is in Christ Jesus ... so that he might be just and the justifier of the one who has faith in Jesus. (Romans 3:23-26)

Here is our own simplified interpretation of these words:

> Everyone has failed God and therefore misses out on his presence, but we are made right with God by his free gift,

32

paid for by Jesus ... In this way, God remains a good judge, while at the same time declaring those who believe in Jesus "not guilty."

This is incredibly good news!

We have all done wrong. None of us should look down on others as "sinners" because we have all sinned. Even if we are good at hiding it, we are all failures. Every other religion tells you how to become a better person by following various rules and rituals. Christianity says your life is in such a mess that you need God Himself to fix it. Surrendering to God's plan for your life is the key to true freedom.

The idea of "falling short" comes from the world of archery. If you aim at a target and your shot doesn't go far enough, your arrow doesn't even reach the target. Even if some of us have a better aim than others, there is still no chance of any of us reaching God's goal of perfection, as we will always *fall short* of His standards.

> Every other religion tells you how to become a better person by following various rules and rituals. Christianity says your life is in such a mess that you need God Himself to fix it.

As a result, we miss out on the "glory" of God, or to put it another way, we are far away from God. Our sin forms a barrier between God and us. There is absolutely nothing we can do ourselves to fix this.

DO YOU REALLY WANT WHAT YOU DESERVE?

Many people say they want "justice." When bad things happen they complain, "This is not fair. I do not deserve this!" You may not have behaved any worse than the next person and wonder why they should have a better life than you. But we have all sinned, and therefore the only thing we all actually deserve is the appropriate penalty: death.

GRACE

An act of undeserved favor motivated by love rather than anything the person who receives this free gift has done to earn or deserve it.

God cannot even look at sinners like us unless we have been made clean (Habakkuk 1:13). Be careful what you ask for. Don't request what you deserve, that is judgment. Instead, appeal for Him to graciously grant that which you have done nothing to earn, that is mercy.

Despite our guilt, God forgives all those who turn to Him, and justifies them, that is, declares them not guilty. There is absolutely nothing in us that motivates God to do this. This act of undeserved favor is called grace, a gift that is neither earned nor deserved. We have done nothing to qualify for it, nor can we ever repay it. God's grace towards us is amazing.

Redemption is a bit like a ransom paid to free a victim of kidnapping. We are so fortunate that Jesus came, and through His death and resurrection, paid the price for us. God redeems you not just from the past, but builds and shapes you back into what you were always supposed to be. God rejoices as each individual is restored to their original purpose.

If we were standing before a judge and knew we were guilty of a crime, we would want to hear the words "not guilty." But, we would have to admit that we owed a debt to society. A judge who simply let us off would not be a good judge, because there would be no justice. God is a holy God and His standard is perfection. Sin offends His perfect nature and cannot simply be ignored.

Our debt needed to be paid. God's innocent Son, Jesus, was the only One who could pay it for us. Through Jesus' death and resurrection, our sins, which the Bible also calls trespasses, were removed. We deserve the punishment of death; Jesus did not. He took our place. A righteous One exchanged for an unrighteous one.

Jesus experienced separation from His Father so that we could be reunited with God. All of our sin was cancelled. The righteous anger of God against sin was turned away. It is now completely just for God to pardon us. What great news!

> Blessed are those whose lawless deeds are forgiven, and whose sins are covered; blessed is the man against whom the Lord will not count his sin. (Romans 4:7-8)

REDEMPTION

Refers to the truth that Jesus came and through His death and resurrection paid the price for our sins and builds and shapes you back into what you were always supposed to be.

> God made [us] alive together with him, having forgiven us all our trespasses, by canceling the record of debt that stood against us with its legal demands. This he set aside, nailing it to the cross. (Colossians 2:13-14)

If you are a Christian, God has wiped all your sins away and you stand before Him "justified," or as some have explained it, *"just as if I'd* never sinned!"

FREE, BUT PROVIDED AT GREAT COST

> God shows his love for us in that while we were still sinners, Christ died for us. (Romans 5:8)

We must never forget what a terrible price was paid for our rescue. Jesus was "delivered up" for our sins (Romans 4:25). He was tortured and cruelly crucified. His anguish at experiencing separation from God the Father is hard for us to comprehend. Jesus' suffering was as infinite as His love is eternal.

The verse continues, He was "raised for our justification." Death could not hold Him. After three days in a tomb He came back to life because, despite paying the price for our sin, He remained the only One who actually deserved to live. He was punished, but not for eternity. As a sign that God had accepted the penalty, He raised Jesus from the dead and, in so doing, Jesus was declared "not guilty" to the whole universe. In a sense He was "justified." This didn't *just* mean that Jesus had never sinned. Rather, it meant He had completed a perfect and sinless life. The Bible calls this righteousness.

Jesus' credit of righteousness has now been applied to the account of every Christian. This is such a large amount that it cancels out all your sins. It is not like you have a clean slate and must now work to impress Him. Jesus' death on the cross has dealt with your sin. His resurrection has provided you with a new life and completely changed the way that God looks at you. God sees you as if you have already completed your life, having obeyed Him at all times. It is as if you are hidden inside the person of Jesus, and when God looks at you, He sees His Son. He sees sinless perfection. He calls you righteous:

> For our sake he made him to be sin who knew no sin, so that in him we might become the righteousness of God. (2 Corinthians 5:21)

Christians were united with Jesus in His death, and our sin died with Him. In His resurrection we have also become a new person in Him. Jesus now lives inside us, renewing us with resurrection power:

> I have been crucified with Christ. It is no longer I who
> live, but Christ who lives in me. (Galatians 2:20)

This new life will last forever. Because Jesus rose again, we
can be sure that one day, all who follow Him will also live
again.

Because of what Jesus did for us, God no longer calls
Christians "sinners." Instead he calls us all "saints," which
means holy ones. We are considered holy people, not because
of anything we have done, but because of Jesus, our Savior.

You may be asking, "If God will keep on forgiving me,
why not just keep on sinning?" If you are thinking this, then
you have understood the remarkable scandal of this message.
There is, however, a very clear answer to this question, which
we will explore later.

First we must ask another critical question: How can
I make sure that I benefit from this good news? How do
I become a Christian? Or, if I once thought I was a Christian,
but have now drifted away from God, how do I find my way
back?

QUESTIONS TO CONSIDER:

1. The Bible says, "All have sinned, and fall short of the glory of God." Do you believe this?

2. Have you committed sins that you regret?

3. Do you believe that all sins can be forgiven?

KEY BIBLE VERSES:

Romans 5:1-11
John 19:17-30
John 20:1-31

3

How do I become a Christian?

The Bible explains the story of humanity and the way God saves us in three stages. This is summarized in the following passage, which is explained in three diagrams on the next page:

> And you were dead in the trespasses and sins in which you once walked, following the course of this world, following the prince of the power of the air, the spirit that is now at work in the sons of disobedience— among whom we all once lived in the passions of our flesh, carrying out the desires of the body and the mind, and were by nature children of wrath, like the rest of mankind. But God, being rich in mercy, because of the great love with which he loved us, even when we were dead in our trespasses, made us alive together with Christ—by grace you have been saved— and raised us up with him and seated us with him in the heavenly places in Christ Jesus, so that in the coming ages he

might show the immeasurable riches of his grace in kindness toward us in Christ Jesus. For by grace you have been saved through faith. And this is not your own doing; it is the gift of God, not a result of works, so that no one may boast. (Ephesians 2:1-9)

STAGE ONE: DEAD IN SIN

GOD

WITHOUT GOD WE ARE:

"dead in trespasses and sins"

"following the course of this world"

"carrying out the desires of the body and the mind"

"by nature children of wrath"

(Ephesians 2:1-3)

We are all trapped in a pit called sin, which separates us from God. Nothing we can do ourselves will ever save us. All our efforts to please God are hopeless.

STAGE TWO: MADE ALIVE

GOD

BUT GOD, WHO IS RICH IN MERCY:

"loved us, even when we were dead"

"made us alive together with Christ."

(Ephesians 2:4-5)

While we are still dead in our sin, Jesus came into our pit to rescue us. Through His death and resurrection Jesus provided us with the only way out.

Many rejected Him, but, "to all who did receive him, who believed in his name, he gave the right to become children of God" (John 1:12).

STAGE THREE: RAISED WITH CHRIST

"raised us up with him"

"seated us with him"

"so that he might show the im-measurable riches of his grace."

(Ephesians 2:6-7)

When someone becomes a Christian, they are made alive with Jesus, who lifts them out of the pit, and he or she is now in a relationship with God.

The above process needs to become real and personal in an individual's life. An example of where a group of people became Christians is found in Acts 2, on the day the Church began.

Early that morning, 120 people made quite a scene as they burst out of a prayer meeting on to the streets of ancient Jerusalem. They were the followers of Jesus who had remained loyal to Him despite His death.

"Drunkards!" someone yelled at them, because they seemed full of joy, almost intoxicated. The Apostle Peter, often the spokesman, answered in their defence that it was surely too early for bars to be open, and gave the true reason for their happiness. He described what a terrible wrong had been committed when Jesus Christ, the Son of God, was tortured and publicly executed. The Savior that the world had been waiting thousands of years for had been rejected in the worst possible way.

It was our sin that drove Jesus to the cross. If we had lived in Jesus' time, we might like to think we would have been part of the crowd that welcomed Him into Jerusalem, singing, "Hosanna to the son of David!" But just days later, the very same crowd shouted, "Crucify him! Crucify him!"

The Apostle Peter's conclusion was remarkable: Jesus had been raised from the dead! He was now seated at God's side in heaven, ruling the universe. Peter's hearers were familiar with how kings in those days would avenge themselves brutally. Full of the sudden realization that they had sinned against God Himself, they asked, *"What shall we do?"*

Peter's reply is compelling in its simplicity, and demonstrates that God is not the kind of person who delights in taking revenge. Strikingly, he explains that God offers mercy and forgiveness, even to the people who had demanded the Romans execute Jesus:

> Repent and be baptized every one of you in the name of Jesus Christ for the forgiveness of your sins, and you will receive the gift of the Holy Spirit ... there were added that day about three thousand souls. (Acts 2:38-41)

In this passage we find four steps that should mark the beginning of the Christian life:

STEPS TO BEGIN YOUR CHRISTIAN LIFE

STEP ONE: REPENT AND BELIEVE

Make a choice to think differently about Jesus and live for Him. This step is broken down into three parts in the following verse:

> If you confess with your mouth that Jesus is Lord and believe in your heart that God raised him from the dead, you will be saved. (Romans 10:9)

a. "Confess with your mouth"

Tell someone you want to become a Christian.

b. "Jesus is Lord"

Choose to worship Jesus as God and follow Him as your Lord.

Admit that you have sinned against Him. Ask Him to forgive you.

c. "Believe in your heart that God raised Jesus from the dead"

Thank Jesus for dying for you and rising from the dead for you.

Once you have decided to follow Jesus, there are three further steps which naturally follow:

STEP TWO: BE BAPTIZED

Make a public declaration of your new faith in Jesus.

STEP THREE: RECEIVE THE GIFT OF THE HOLY SPIRIT

Be empowered to live your new life as a Christian.

Step Four: Be Added to a Church
Become part of Jesus' family.

These steps will be explained in the rest of this chapter and the next.

Step One: Repent and Believe

Make a choice to think differently about Jesus and live for Him. This first step underpins all the others. The word "repent" is not often used today. There are four components to what it means: a change of *mind*, a change of *heart*, a change of *behavior*, and a change of *direction*.

Repentance means changing what you think about Jesus, and apologizing for ignoring Him, belittling Him, excluding Him, and not trusting Him. It is a radical change in perspective.

> ### Repentance
> A change of mind, a change of heart, a change of behavior, and a change of direction.
>
> Often used interchangeably with "believe", but involves more than mere intellectual assent.

Repentance involves your heart being miraculously renewed so that you now love and value Jesus above everything else and are satisfied in Him.

Repentance includes turning from your sins. However, Christianity is not primarily external behavior, but an internal conversion. The outer works flow from the inner work. Repentance means reorienting your life around Jesus, and asking Him to rescue you and to be in charge from now on. It means changing from a life that is all about you, to a life that is all about Jesus.

Repentance is such a simple concept, yet it does demand that your whole life change direct-ion. You stop going your own way, and turn around; you convert. You must count the cost of such a decision. But the choice is between living your own way forever, apart from God and under His judgment, or following Jesus and enjoying His presence. Jesus warned us often that hell is a real place (e.g. Matthew 10:28). Why would anyone want to end up there?

Sometimes repentance can be accompanied by strong emotions, but the key element is a sober decision to start on a lifetime of following Jesus:

> For godly grief produces a repentance that leads to salvation without regret, whereas worldly grief produces death. (2 Corinthians 7:10)

In some of the other messages recorded in Acts, hearers are urged to "believe" in place of the word "repent" (see Acts 15:7 and Acts 16:31). While repentance is about more than just agreeing with certain truths, it does begin with what we must believe:

> If you confess with your mouth that Jesus is Lord and believe in your heart that God raised him from the dead, you will be saved. (Romans 10:9)

According to this verse there are three components to the decision to believe in and trust Jesus, which is at the heart of repentance:

The first is that you must openly say something, or "confess with your mouth."

The second, is *what* you must say: "Jesus is Lord."

The third, is what you must "believe in your heart": God has raised Jesus from the dead.

This is how to begin the Christian life. Without this response you will never be saved. With it, even if what the Bible calls "fruits in keeping with repentance" (Luke 3:8) are not yet visible in your life, you can be sure that they will begin to appear.

Let's look at each of these components of our response to the gospel in more detail:

A. "CONFESS WITH YOUR MOUTH"
Tell someone you want to become a Christian.
The idea behind this phrase is similar to a marriage service, where a couple declares their commitment to a lifelong relationship with one another. Some people argue that marriage is an unnecessary piece of paper. But we are changeable beings, and in years to come it is helpful to have a memory of the day we acknowledged our love before other people. Also, something actually changes inside us when we openly make such a declaration.

In the same way, we must tell God, ourselves, and other people that we will now follow Jesus. This solidifies our commitment to a relationship with God and transforms us. It is very possible to become a Christian right now in private. But you will need to tell somebody, and as soon as possible. Usually another Christian will be the best person to tell first.

Many new Christians feel so full of love for Jesus that they want everyone else to share in their newfound joy. Despite our enthusiasm and passion to tell others, there are times when you need to be wise about who you tell and how.

The biblical account of Esther is interesting in this regard. Esther was a Jew living in exile in a hostile country. When she was taken to the king's palace Mordecai wisely advised her not to tell anyone that she was a member of God's people (Esther 2:10). If she had, she might well have been instantly killed. At the right time, in the right way, when Esther admitted her identity to the king, it led to a miraculous rescue of her people from genocide (Esther 7:3-4 and 8:4-12).

It may help you to find a mature Christian to talk through the wisest steps for you to take as you begin to tell others about your new faith, especially if you are concerned about negative consequences. Pray that God will help you know who to tell, and when.

It is sometimes hard to say, "I am a Christian." However, to do so is liberating. There comes a point in everybody's faith journey when what may have happened secretly in their heart must be declared openly. In fact, telling somebody that we now believe is an essential part of becoming a Christian. Jesus also warns,

> Everyone who acknowledges me before men, I also will acknowledge before my Father who is in heaven, but whoever denies me before men, I also will deny before my Father who is in heaven. (Matthew 10:32-33)

B. "Jesus is Lord"

Choose to worship Him as God and follow Him as your Lord. Admit that you have sinned against Him. Ask Him to forgive you.

There is rich meaning in these three words. The word "Lord" is used all over the New Testament as a name for God. At the heart of Christianity lies the belief that Jesus is God, and following His triumphant resurrection, He is the ruler of the universe who will one day return to earth to reign as King.

The Christian God is three in one: God the Father, God the Son, and

TRINITY

The word used to summarize the Christian belief that God has always existed as a loving community of three distinct persons: The Father, The Son, and The Holy Spirit. Together they form one God, not three gods.

47

God the Holy Spirit. The Apostle John begins his Gospel by saying that Jesus, who he calls, "The Word," *is* God: "In the beginning was the Word, and the Word was with God, and the Word was God" (John 1:1).

Christians explain this by the concept of the Trinity: God has always existed as three persons, but one God, and we worship them all. Perhaps one of the clearest demonstrations of their personhood was at Jesus' baptism, when they each had distinct roles. The Son was the one getting wet, the Father spoke from heaven, and the Spirit appeared in the form of a dove (Luke 3:21-22).

The Bible tells us that "God is love" by His very nature (1 John 4:16). This was true even when only the Trinity existed, and there was no one else to love. God has eternally been a community of three people, and so we should never foolishly imagine that He was lonely before the universe was created.

From eternity past the members of the Trinity have loved and indwelt each other. Jesus said, "The Father is in me and I am in the Father" (John 10:38).

There are several illustrations commonly used to describe God. While these are all helpful to some extent, they all have weaknesses which help us realize what God is *not* like.

The Trinity is often compared to water, which can exist in three forms: liquid, steam, and ice. However, God is not sometimes the Father, sometimes the Son, and sometimes the Holy Spirit. He is all three all at once.

Another illustration that is used is a man who may be simultaneously a husband, a father, and a son. However, the man is only one person, who functions in different ways. In contrast, God comprises three persons, rather than three manifestations of the same person.

Ultimately, God is incomparable and all we can finally do is worship Him. The three persons of the Trinity are distinct from each other, yet together they make up one God. This truth has been expressed

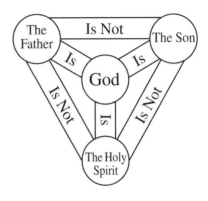

for centuries in a diagram we include on this page. This is a profound mystery. Yet it is a simple truth.

Calling Jesus "Lord" also declares that He is in charge of you and that you will live for Him. Many today do not want to surrender the control of their lives to *anyone*, let alone to Jesus. The Bible is clear: you cannot be a Christian and carry on living for yourself. If Jesus is your Lord, you must obey Him and give Him your total allegiance.

How you choose to respond to Jesus is the most important decision you will ever make. Some say, "He was a great teacher, the best the world has ever seen." Even secular historians recognize that Jesus was the most influential man in all of history. Others go further saying, "He was a great prophet." But Jesus claimed to be God, accepted worship, and proclaimed that He would rise from the dead. Good teachers don't claim they are the only way to God; instead, they point to their teachings. What He said was either true, or else He was foolish, or a liar. Jesus, it is often said, was either bad, mad, or God.

If you are not yet a Christian, recognizing Jesus as God and choosing to worship and follow Him as your Lord is the crucial turning point. Declaring Jesus to be your Lord and meaning it requires the help of the Holy Spirit (1 Corinthians 12:3).

It is crucial that you admit to Jesus that you have sinned, and ask Him to forgive you, and help you to follow Him from now on.

Tell Jesus about your life: the good, the bad, and the ugly. Recognize that you have lived your way with no reference to Him. Specifically list and repent of all your sins. Thank Him for promising to forgive you, even for the sins you have forgotten to confess.

Invite Jesus into your life. Ask Him to take full control, not coming as a friend but as your master. Surrender all authority to Him.

C. "Believe in your heart that God raised Jesus from the dead."

Thank Him for dying for you and rising from the dead for you.

One definition of a Christian is: "Someone who believes in the physical resurrection of Jesus from the dead, and lives their life in light of the implications of that event."

The idea that Jesus' physical resurrected body left behind an empty tomb is the foundation of Christianity. Why would we follow a dead man?

Only Jesus' resurrection could have convinced the frightened disciples to begin the fastest growing movement the world has ever known. They did not gain riches, fame, or power, but rather persecution, torture and death, and yet none of them denied their faith. Nothing other than Jesus' resurrection can make sense of the phenomenal growth and persistence of the Church throughout the ages, despite many attempts to stamp it out.

Almost anywhere you go in the world today you will meet Christians. They worship in different ways, and even believe some different things. But they all agree that Jesus rose again, He is alive!

There is no more important question than, "Did Jesus rise from the dead?" This is the foundation on which the Christian faith stands or falls. As Paul explains, if Jesus were still dead then we would have no hope (1 Corinthians 15:14-19).

If you find the idea of Jesus conquering death and leaving behind an empty tomb difficult to believe, ask God to reveal the truth to you. An article which examines the evidence for Jesus' resurrection is available free online at **adrianwarnock. com/resurrection.**

If you want to become a Christian you must change your mind about Jesus, and accept Him as the risen Lord. God does not ask you to repent, become perfect, and then one day He might be pleased with you. He promises that if you simply trust in Him, then He accepts you already.

The most quoted verse in the Bible promises us that if we have faith in Jesus we will live forever with Him:

> For God so loved the world, that he gave his only Son, that whoever believes in him should not perish but have eternal life. (John 3:16)

CONCLUSION

We hope this chapter has made it clear that becoming a Christian is neither learned nor earned. It is a free gift from God.

This is the simple gospel message. Don't let anyone tell you it is more complicated than this:

> Everyone who calls on the name of the Lord will be saved. (Romans 10:13)

If you are ready to become a Christian right now, pray to Jesus:

Thank Jesus for dying for you on the cross.

Tell Him you believe in His resurrection.

Talk to Jesus about your past, the good and the bad.

Repent of your sins by asking Him for forgiveness.

Acknowledge Jesus as Lord of your life and tell Him that you will worship Him.

Invite Him to take control of your life and live in you.

Tell Jesus that you will now follow Him for the rest of your life.

If you prayed something like this, and believed it in your heart, you are now a Christian, and may we be the first to welcome you into God's family.

Who will you tell first?

KEY BIBLE VERSES:

Acts 2:37-41
Romans 10:9-13
John 3:1-21

4

Next Steps: What do I do now?

It is very possible to know a lot about the Bible, and to even go to church without ever having had a real relationship with Jesus. I (Tope) was once like that. As a young man, I knew a lot about the Bible. I was familiar with its stories, and some of its characters, because I read it recreationally. I would even arrogantly try to embarrass Christians who spoke to me by demonstrating they did not know the contents as much as I did. But the fact remained; I had never had a real encounter with Jesus. I had not asked Him to save me. I suppose I was a little bit like the Pharisee we spoke about in chapter one.

One day I accompanied my sister to a church that met in a movie theater. I was sure *she* needed to be saved. But that day God also had plans for me. I don't really remember what the preacher said. I do remember an appeal was given inviting anyone who wanted to know Jesus to come forward. I didn't want to raise my hand in response, or go to the front. But sitting in my seat I became very aware of the reality of who God is, and the sinner that I was. I felt like I had been somehow brought to a moment of decision. I invited Jesus into my life. It was at that point that I had a real encounter with Him.

From that point on everything began to change. Portions of the Bible that I had read as stories became far more meaningful and alive to me. They no longer felt like fables recorded, or merely words on a page. They became life-giving truth to me, and food for my soul. I found they gave me help, and established my assurance that I was a Christian.

Later on I learned about Jesus' clear command in the Bible that we should be baptized. The church I attended explained what this meant to me, and I decided to be baptized because I wanted to follow Jesus in His example and in His instructions. So one day I was baptized by immersion in water, and joined a church. This is how my journey with God began.

Many people ask, "What is the minimum I can do in order to become a Christian?" But they risk missing out on some of what God intends for us to receive.

In the last chapter we discussed true repentance or faith: that is, turning from your own way to believe in Jesus as Lord. This is the only requirement to becoming a Christian. But Peter does not stop there; he outlines two further steps, which flow from repentance, and are meant to mark the beginning of your Christian life. A fourth step is also mentioned a few verses later. We will explore all these steps in this chapter.

Certain things are meant to accompany saving faith and demonstrate that it is real. As simple as this idea of repentance is, it has massive implications. The Apostle Peter told his listeners that the first action flowing from repentance is to be baptized.

STEP TWO: BE BAPTIZED

MAKE A PUBLIC DECLARATION OF YOUR NEW FAITH IN JESUS.

As we discussed in the last chapter, making a public confession of your faith is very important. If you have never been baptized, the best way to openly declare your faith is to invite your friends and family to witness you following the command of both the Apostle Peter and the Lord Jesus Himself. Your baptism will be a vivid demonstration of the gospel to those closest to you, as well as a crucial moment in your walk with God.

Baptism is a way of publicly demonstrating the reality of what God has done for you in your heart. It doesn't make you a Christian any more than jogging makes you human. But just as running is a sign that you are alive, baptism is a good sign you have made Jesus your Lord.

The word "baptism" literally means to be immersed or dunked. Bible verses talk of "much water" being required (John 3:23), and of going "down into" and "up out of" the water (Acts 8:36-39). We believe these verses demonstrate that baptism in New Testament times meant to get soaked, like in a bath, in the same way that Jesus was baptized by being immersed in the river Jordan.

We believe that the biblical pattern for baptism is to submerge in water people who have chosen to follow Jesus for themselves. However, there are many genuine Christians who have a different view of this, so some churches will instead sprinkle water on the head, as in the case of an infant. They do this because they feel that verses like Genesis 17:7 and Acts 2:38-39 show that God blesses families as a whole unit, and so the children of believers are part of God's covenant community. It seems to us, however, that in the book of Acts

55

baptism follows the faith of the individual being baptized. So, for example, when the Philippian jailer and his whole family were baptized, this was after they had *all* listened to the gospel message, and believed it, and their newfound faith led to them all being full of joy (Acts 16:30-34).

Christians may differ on the when and the how, but one thing that we can all agree on is that Christians should be baptized, and that making a public profession of your faith in Jesus is a critically important step in your life as a believer in Christ.

Jesus gave very clear instructions to His followers after His resurrection:

> Go therefore and make disciples of all nations, baptizing them in the name of the Father and of the Son and of the Holy Spirit, teaching them to observe all that I have commanded you. (Matthew 28:19-20)

BAPTISM

An act of obedience to Jesus that demonstrates publicly the reality of what God has done in your heart. It marks a turning away from your old life and the beginning of your new.

It would be very strange to claim that you want to follow Jesus as your Lord, but then refuse to obey the first command He gives you after you have repented.

Jesus Himself was baptized (Luke 3:21-22), despite the fact that He had never sinned. Sometimes people feel that they have become a Christian too recently to be baptized, or that they have followed Jesus for so long it now seems pointless and too late. But there is no better time than right now to follow Jesus' example.

Baptism is all about turning from your old life and beginning a new one. It is a way of demonstrating that you are now seeking to follow Jesus. It is "for the forgiveness of your sins" (Acts 2:38), and represents a bath to wash away our sins:

> Baptism ... now saves you, not as a removal of dirt from the body but as an appeal to God for a good conscience, through the resurrection of Jesus Christ. (1 Peter 3:21)

Through baptism we identify with both the death and resurrection of Jesus. It is like our own death, burial, and funeral service. We die to our old way of life by sharing in Jesus' death. Baptism by immersion demonstrates this visually. As a person goes down under the water, it is as if they have been buried:

> All of us who have been baptized into Christ Jesus were baptized into his death. (Romans 6:3)

As a person comes up out of the water, this represents the way that Jesus has raised them up to a new life, a new beginning:

> Having been buried with him in baptism, in which you were also raised with him through faith in the powerful working of God, who raised him from the dead. (Colossians 2:12)

> Therefore, if anyone is in Christ, he is a new creation. The old has passed away; behold, the new has come. (2 Corinthians 5:17)

Baptism represents our certain hope that while we will still experience physical death (unless Jesus returns first), God will not leave us in the grave. Instead, Jesus will raise us up to live with Him forever. We will have renewed bodies and we will finally meet our Savior face-to-face (1 Corinthians 13:12).

There is a supernatural element to baptism. It is more than an outward ritual. It is truly a fresh start, and represents a clear cutting off and freedom from unhelpful ties to the past. Christians will often experience an inner feeling of being made "new." Just as God said to Jesus, "This is my beloved Son," when He was baptized, many Christians report feeling the love of God in a tangible way at the moment of their baptism.

When you are baptized, your local church is also declaring before God and witnesses that they believe you are now a Christian. Don't be surprised if the church you attend wants to get to know you a little first, or if they ask you to attend a preparation course. It can sometimes be a little frustrating to wait once you have made up your mind, but Jesus sees your heart and the desire you have to obey Him in this way.

In the next step, the Apostle Peter promises to those who repent and are baptized, "you will receive the gift of the Holy Spirit" (Acts 2:38).

STEP THREE: RECEIVE THE GIFT OF THE HOLY SPIRIT

BE EMPOWERED TO LIVE YOUR NEW LIFE AS A CHRISTIAN.

The Holy Spirit is very much God. He is not a force or a power, but a person. As such, the Apostle Peter invites everybody who has repented and turned to Jesus to also receive the Holy Spirit.

The Holy Spirit is at work in every Christian, not just a select few. We learn in John 3:8 that the Holy Spirit causes us to be born again. Indeed, the Holy Spirit is at work in you even before you decide to become a Christian, showing you your sin, and drawing you to Jesus (John 16:8).

Every Christian has Jesus living inside of them by the Holy Spirit. Christ's resurrection power is at work in us all, transforming us from the inside out, and producing the fruit of the Spirit (Galatians 5:22-23).

When Peter talks here about "receiving" the Holy Spirit into our lives, this refers to us becoming aware of the Spirit as a person, and entering a relationship with Him.

Like the wind, we cannot see the Spirit, but we can see evidence of His presence by what He is doing. However, we can experience the work of the Holy Spirit in a dynamic way. The Bible invites us to "be filled with the Holy Spirit" (Ephesians 5:18). The tense of the verb is continuous so it could also be translated "be being filled." Other verses which also suggest being filled with the Spirit is not a once-for-all thing include Ephesians 1:17 and 3:19, Colossians 1:11, Acts 4:8, 4:31, 13:9 and 13:52. All Christians are invited to consciously, and continuously welcome the Holy Spirit, and invite Him to work in our lives.

Jesus promised to give the Holy Spirit to anyone who comes to Him:

> On the last day of the feast, the great day, Jesus stood up and cried out, "If anyone thirsts, let him come to me and drink. Whoever believes in me, as the Scripture has said, 'Out of his heart will flow rivers of living water.'" Now this he said about the Spirit, whom those who believed in him were to receive, for as yet the Spirit had not been given, because Jesus was not yet glorified. (John 7:37-39)

It is very possible to become a Christian without much in the way of an emotional experience. We are not saved because we cried, or because something dramatic happened. Everybody's story is different. However, over time, you will become aware of the effects of the Holy Spirit's work in you, some of which are outlined as follows:

An enabling to speak about Jesus with others

The disciples had been told to wait in Jerusalem until they received power from the Holy Spirit to take the gospel all over the world (Acts 1:8). He equips and empowers us in all kinds of ways to serve God, and gives us boldness to do works for God today (Acts 4:31).

A feeling of inclusion among God's people

The Holy Spirit confirms that you are really a Christian:

> And because you are sons, God has sent the Spirit of his Son into our hearts, crying, "Abba! Father!" (Galatians 4:6)

The outpouring of the Spirit is one of the marks that identify God's people (Acts 2:39). We are born into His family, and the Holy Spirit gives us a sense of belonging. No longer does God's Spirit only rest on specific individuals as in Old Testament times; now He is available to everyone.

A restored relationship with God

Through the Holy Spirit, God speaks to our hearts. He lives within us. "God's love has been poured into our hearts through the Holy Spirit who has been given to us" (Romans 5:5).

There is so much more that the Holy Spirit can do for you if you ask.

> It is very possible to become a Christian without much in the way of an emotional experience.

The work of the Spirit will further establish you in your walk with God. You will grow in the fruit of the Spirit (Galatians 5).

We encourage you to find out more about Him, and to invite the Spirit to work in you to glorify Jesus, revealing Him to you (John 16:14).

STEP FOUR: BE ADDED TO A CHURCH

BECOME PART OF JESUS' FAMILY.

It is easy to miss the fact that on the same day that the Apostle Peter urged the crowd to repent, be baptized, and receive the Holy Spirit, those who accepted God's Word also joined a church.

The Bible knows nothing of solo Christianity, but encourages us to be devoted to one another as a family:

> So those who received his word were baptized, and there were added that day about three thousand souls. And they devoted themselves to the apostles' teaching and the fellowship, to the breaking of bread and the prayers. (Acts 2:41-42)

It is important to find a church where you can fellowship, or to use a more modern word, be in partnership with other believers. A new Christian becomes part of God's kingdom and there is a way to live in that kingdom. A good church will support you as you learn how to do that, and help you to prize Jesus above everything.

The church community will demonstrate Jesus' love to you. Whether it is large or small, the church you attend should feel like a family where people care for and look out for each other.

You will need a lot of advice and support from Christian friends as you learn to serve Jesus. But over time you will also benefit from opportunities to help others. Every Christian has a specific job from Jesus to do. Being in a church is how that is worked out. Christians are together not to form a comfortable club, but to play our unique part in God's mission:

> For we are his workmanship, created in Christ Jesus for
> good works, which God prepared beforehand, that we
> should walk in them. (Ephesians 2:10)

Join a church where worshipping Jesus is a priority. The style
of music is less important than the attitude of the heart. You
need to be a part of a church where everything really is all
about Jesus.

A good church will have preaching and small groups to
help you understand the Bible. Join a church which honors
the Word of God, and approaches it humbly, as discussed further in chapter 6. Like Paul's hearers, you will also need to
examine God's Word yourself to confirm that what you are
hearing is actually based on the Scriptures:

> They received the word with all eagerness, examining the
> Scriptures daily to see if these things were so. (Acts 17:11)

Prayer is vital to the life of a Christian because it is the way
Christians communicate with God. Make sure that you find
a church where there are opportunities for you to pray with
others. There is nothing that will help you more in your relationship with God than to learn how to pray.

Christians everywhere form one united Body, and so it
is vital that churches relate to one another. Ask your leaders
which other churches they are partners with, and be sure that
they are not completely isolated from other believers.

The Christian life is like a journey. There are a number
of things that you can do to help you on your way. Joining
a good church is at the top of that list.

If you don't already attend a church, start looking. God
will help you find one that takes the Bible seriously, and loves
people.

QUESTIONS TO CONSIDER:

1. Do you need to be baptized?

2. Do you regularly ask Jesus to fill you with the Holy Spirit?

3. Have you found a church yet? If not, how are you going to go about finding one?

KEY BIBLE VERSES:

Colossians 2:6-15
John 1:1-18

5

You can Change

Many years ago, I (Adrian) knew a man who appeared to be a strong Christian. Every week he eagerly attended the same church I did. One day the man simply stopped coming. None of my friends knew why, and some even reached out to him, but no one got anywhere.

Months later, as suddenly as he had left, the man came back. He explained he had decided to no longer live as a Christian because he had begun a sexual relationship outside of marriage. However, he had been uncomfortable with that decision, and throughout that time, he described feeling almost as if a parrot was on his shoulder saying, "I'm still here and I still love you!" He admitted this had been frankly annoying. All he wanted to do was forget Jesus. But he couldn't shake off what he now understood was the presence of God. Many of us were in tears as he told the church he would now no longer resist God, but rather follow Him.

Most people have an instinctive idea of how Christians "should" behave. Often new Christians find some of their friends will suddenly stop swearing around them, and may be too embarrassed to speak about their Friday night activities.

Meanwhile, many Christians assume that they must become religious. Sadly, many well-meaning churches unwittingly impose a long list of rules and obligations, which can overshadow the message of undeserved grace. Some find this so-called "Christian lifestyle" impossible to sustain and drift away, slowly turning their backs on Jesus. Tragically, they have gone about it the wrong way.

If you too have wandered away from God, then He is waiting for you to simply take a step back toward Him, like the father in the story of the prodigal son (Luke 15:11-32).

Until we understand our new identity in Jesus we will constantly struggle with feelings of condemnation, and keep repeating the same mistakes. Real Christianity is not about what we do, but about what Jesus has already done for us, and what He promises to do in and through us.

Some other Christians presume on the wonderful news of forgiveness. They ask themselves, "If God will forgive me no matter what, surely I can keep on living as I please, can't I?" The Apostle Paul answered a similar question with a forceful, "By no means!" (Romans 6:1-2). We have died to our old way of life and been united with Jesus in a new life that will last forever. Jesus has broken the power of sin inside us, even though it may not feel that way at times. How can we live as though nothing has happened?

> When Jesus says, "Follow me," it's not like on Twitter where you simply press a button. He wants your whole life.

The only appropriate response to unconditional forgiveness is to decide to follow Jesus. God did not save us in order for us to carry on sinning. Christians are not made faultless. We do still sin, but we never feel comfortable afterwards.

When Jesus says, "Follow me," it's not like on Twitter where you simply press a button. He wants your whole life. Deciding to follow Jesus is not just about escaping eternal punishment; it is about changing your way of life.

Becoming a Christian involves a radical change of heart. This happens when you truly receive the good news of what Jesus has done for you and turn to Him. You no longer have to worry about whether or not God is pleased with you. Your guilt has been removed. He is delighted with you. He actually *likes* you. He invites you to be with Him for eternity. His love is so great that He will accept you even when you sin again.

God loves us so much that He wants to guide us through our lives for His glory and our fulfillment. He knows what is best for us because He designed us. He created us with the purpose that we should love Him as well as other people. Jesus said it is better to give than to receive (Acts 20:35). In other words, a selfish life is far inferior to living for the good of others.

As a Christian you do not need to work to earn God's favor. But because Jesus has done so much for you, you love Him, and choose to follow Him, eager to please Him by the things that you say and do.

CHANGE BEGINS WITH A DEEP-ROOTED RESPONSE TO THE GOSPEL

Perhaps you have recently heard a sermon that led you to decide to become a Christian. It is vital that this response becomes a whole-hearted change of direction that affects every aspect of your life. The gospel contains the power of God to save people. But this is only brought into effect when you truly believe the message (Romans 1:16).

If you want to become a Christian you must make a firm decision to give your life to the Lord. From then on, you know that you are not perfect, but that you are saved. God has accepted you, and this does not change when you sin, or when your feelings condemn you. The Bible calls this moment being "born again" (see John 3:1-8).

When you are born again, your desires radically change. At heart you no longer want to live for yourself, even though at times you feel torn between what Jesus wants for you and the things you previously lived for.

A vague, half-hearted response to the gospel is not the same as being born again. We urge you to consider whether you are really a Christian:

> Examine yourselves, to see whether you are in the faith. Test yourselves. Or do you not realize this about yourselves, that Jesus Christ is in you? – unless indeed you fail to meet the test! (2 Corinthians 13:5)

Some people say they have been born again, but there is absolutely no change in them. Jesus and the true Christian have been united. We are one, and by His Spirit, Jesus lives inside us to transform us. How could all that be true of someone who is still exactly the same as before?

Other people proudly point to the fact that they have become more moral. But living as a Christian involves so much more than stopping certain sins. Real change is not only about turning away from things, but also turning *toward* God.

Real joy can only be found in following Jesus. Being born again is about having been touched by God and responding to Him. It is not enough to merely hear God's Word. The real test is in how we respond to it. Jesus explains this in the following parable:

> A sower went out to sow. And as he sowed, some seeds fell along the path, and the birds came and devoured them. Other seeds fell on rocky ground, where they did not have much soil, and immediately they sprang up, since they had no depth of soil, but when the sun rose they were scorched. And since they had no root, they withered away. Other seeds fell among thorns, and the thorns grew up and choked them. Other seeds fell on good soil and produced grain, some a hundredfold, some sixty, some thirty. (Matthew 13:3-8)

The seed represents God's Word, which can come through reading the Bible, or a Christian book, speaking with friends, or listening to sermons. The Bible has the power to transform, but this isn't released automatically. Just hearing the words is not enough.

The soil in the parable represents the attitude of our hearts. What kind of soil are you going to be? The same seed touches different types of ground. There is no problem with the seed. The issue is with our hearts. When the ground is hard, the seed cannot grow. Some people listen, but don't truly grasp the message. It is quickly forgotten. When people do not fully receive the Word, our enemy snatches it away. It is as though they had never heard it.

Others receive the good news with much emotion. Tears may flow. Great joy may result. The seed takes root and grows quickly. They appear to have become a Christian and are enthusiastic. These people like the good news of Jesus, but their response is short-lived. The ground is too shallow; without deep roots the plant simply withers away.

Jesus warns that a superficial acceptance of the Word is not enough. Some people follow Jesus for what they think they will get out of Him. They treat God like a heavenly slot machine: "If I put in the right amount of prayer and live a good life, I will get everything I want." If it looks like God has failed them because of difficult times, they then reject Him as quickly as they accepted Him.

Jesus told us that we will all face troubles in this world. You will not be protected from all the problems of life. When you become a Christian, your problems do not disappear. When you are in the middle of a season of difficulty, how will you respond? If your faith is deep-rooted, you will draw closer to Jesus. But if you are like the shallow soil, you will soon withdraw from Him. In the same breath that He warns us that we will face various kinds of trials at different times, Jesus comforts us by saying, "Take heart; I have overcome the world" (John 16:33). He will always be with us.

> The same seed touches different types of ground. There is no problem with the seed. The issue is with our hearts.

Some seed was sown among thorns, which represents the "cares of this world" and the "deceitfulness of riches." Jesus warns that it is hard for rich people to enter heaven. If you have food to eat every day, clean water to drink, and safe housing in which to be sheltered, you are rich compared to most of the world.

Surprisingly, though, increased material comfort is usually accompanied by increased worry. So many of us rush about buying the latest gadgets, nice clothes, and home improvements, constantly checking Twitter and Facebook, or pursuing our careers. These things often choke faith. Do you serve the god of money, reputation, or power? God refuses to be your servant in order to fulfil your selfish desires.

Freedom comes from clearing out the thorns, and resolving not to live for the temporary pleasures of this world. Jesus urges us to "seek first the kingdom of God" (Matthew 6:33), which means living for Him rather than for ourselves. Amazingly, He then promises that if we put Him first, we will be blessed and receive everything we truly need. If you devote yourself to Jesus, the things you desire will begin to match with His will. Your striving to better yourself will decrease, and over time, God will teach you how to be content in every situation (Philippians 4:11-13).

Good soil allows the seed to grow, and represents real salvation. It is not adopting a moral lifestyle and following mere religion. It is not going to church and going through the motions. It is not trying to get on the right side of God by doing certain things. Many people live apparently good lives, but their hearts have not been changed. Some are model Christians in the way they live, but inwardly they are full of bitterness and resentment. If you want to be like good soil you must humbly receive the Word, grasping it in the core of your heart, and allow it to bear fruit in your life.

Any child who knows he is loved wants to please his parents. He knows that even though he is naughty at times, and there are consequences for that, it does not change how much he is loved. This is exactly the same in our relationship with God. If you can grasp how much he loves you, confidence and security will be the result.

A healthy tree cannot bear bad fruit, nor can a diseased tree bear good fruit. Every tree that does not bear good fruit is cut down and thrown into the fire. Thus you will recognize them by their fruits. (Matthew 7:18-20)

An apple tree that is well looked after will always produce apples. It will never produce oranges. There is no need for the tree to strain itself since making fruit is in the tree's nature. In the same way, we do not need to strive to try and force ourselves to change in our own strength. Instead, we must learn to draw on the power of God inside us, and the fruit of behavior that is consistent with our new nature will be the result.

We must recognize how helpless we are to change ourselves. Our own efforts are wearisome and lead to condemnation and burnout. As Jesus said, "It is the Spirit who gives life; the flesh is no help at all" (John 6:63). We need God to transform us from the inside out.

If you have absolutely no passion for God and there has been no discernable change in your life, you are probably not saved. Jesus warns us there will be many who call Him "Lord," but He will one day reply, "I never knew you; depart from me, you workers of lawlessness" (Matthew 7:21-23).

Pretending to have faith while doing whatever you want mocks God. There are many false prophets today who bring false messages, which lead to false salvation. The last thing any true pastor wants is for a church member to believe they are on their way to heaven when they are actually on their way to hell.

Do you *know* Jesus? Is there a connection between you and Him? Is there any interaction? Do you love Him as your greatest treasure? This is a matter of eternal life or eternal death. We urge you to ask God right now, "Show me, am I saved?" Make sure of your faith.

Acknowledge that God is God and you are not. He is calling for your heart, not religious observance. We must move beyond an awareness of God to an acknowledgement of God. We must move beyond mere religion to a relationship with Jesus. Religion is destroying more people than anything else. Our own good works can never save us. We can only be saved by the finished work of Jesus.

Jesus warns us that there are two routes we choose from as we live our lives (Matthew 7:13-14). One is a wide and easy road, which leads to disaster, but many people choose it. The other is narrow, and seems difficult, but there is help available. Only this route leads to eternal life. Few choose this way. Resolve to follow Jesus, even if none of your friends do. Take the narrow path.

> The good news is that real salvation is permanent. If you are a child of God, He won't disown you.

Walking along the wide road is so easy. As well as those who are obviously not Christians, it also includes some churchgoers. Some people don't bother to read the Bible, thinking their pastors do it for them. They don't sing in church, preferring to watch the worship band. They don't even pray, congratulating themselves for turning up to meetings, but never actually getting to know Jesus for themselves.

The good news is that genuine salvation is permanent. If you are a child of God, He won't disown you. You can know you are His child by what is inside your heart. Because of what the Lord has done for you, you give yourself to Him. When you sin you regret it and want to do better, and are drawn back to God by His unconditional love. Grace meets you where you are and starts from there.

WHAT DOES TRUE SALVATION LOOK LIKE?

Becoming a Christian involves a decision to respond to Jesus as God. Christians worship Jesus. True salvation means that Christ lives in you. In Isaiah 6:7, God didn't say to the prophet, "You're not as bad as you think you are." Nor did He say, "Get away from me." Rather, He assured him, "Your guilt is taken away!" God says the same thing to everyone who has truly called on Jesus. He promises, "I will give you a new heart, and a new spirit I will put within you" (Ezekiel 36:26). This inevitably changes you.

Christians choose to obey Jesus because we have faith in Him, and believe His ways are right. We make a decision to receive Jesus' Word as truth. We determine to listen to what He says. We resolve to serve God, with our whole bodies given as a sacrifice to Him (Romans 12:1).

God does not want to ruin your fun. His ways are wise and are designed for your good. Sin may seem attractive in the short-term, but temporary pleasure is the enemy of the long-term benefits of following Jesus. You do not have to suffer the bitterness and regret caused by a life spent looking out only for yourself.

Becoming a Christian is also a decision to reject the world as dead to you. This is not a cheap salvation. You are called to lay down your life:

> Jesus is in debt to nobody.

"I have been crucified with Christ" (Galatians 2:20). It is as though you have become like a corpse with no rights. It is impossible to hurt a corpse. You choose to gladly sacrifice everything for the delight of knowing Jesus, and to obey Him despite the cost.

This may sound like a massive sacrifice, and at times you will be called to make difficult decisions. But knowing Jesus outweighs everything else. Jesus is in debt to nobody. He rewards everyone who gives up something for Him.

God raises you up and gives you a wonderful new life. He gives you a new heart so you can enjoy Him and want to follow His ways: It's a miracle deep inside. He lives in all believers, empowering us: "The life I now live in the flesh I live by faith in the Son of God, who loved me and gave himself for me" (Galatians 2:20).

All this will lead to true change, which the Bible calls sanctification. This does not happen overnight. Instead it is a gradual, progressive revolution. None of us will ever arrive at perfection in this life, but we all continue to grow and develop. We are transformed "from one degree of glory to another" (2 Corinthians 3:18), and become more and more like Jesus. We make mistakes along the way, but Jesus always loves us, and is ready to help us.

Christians keep believing God despite hurts, disappointments, and failures. We keep trusting in Him, even when we are in need or going through difficulties. Over time we find that our desires, choices, and actions change. People may start to notice and ask, "What happened to you?"

How do I change?

"Do not be conformed to this world, but be transformed by the renewal of your mind" (Romans 12:2). J. B. Phillips translated this, "Don't let the world squeeze you into its mould." The Greek word translated "transformed" is the root of the word metamorphosis. This is when a caterpillar, which can often be dismissed as "ugly," changes into a beautiful butterfly. What once crawled now flies. Over time the same thing happens to all Christians: everything changes.

The Christian life is an ongoing exercise in what the Bible calls repentance. Repentance starts the moment you decide you want to become a Christian. It continues every day for the rest of your life as you live for Jesus.

There are two errors that you can fall into when it comes to change. The first is to presume that change is automatic and to wait for a magical transformation to happen. The popular phrase, "Let go and let God," couldn't be further from the truth. Some new Christians do notice some immediate and dramatic changes in their desires and behavior. But even for them, other areas in their lives will change more gradually.

The second error is to think we must do all the work ourselves. This leads to legalism, which is empty religious behavior, and can be very damaging. Legalists become ever more strict with themselves, and judgmental toward others.

Putting a "hedge" around sin to make it less likely for us to fall into it may seem sensible, but the important question is, "What is in your heart?" If your efforts turn you into a Pharisee, then Jesus will not be impressed at all. Rules and regulations do not restrict sin; instead they often promote it. When you see a sign that reads, "Do not walk on the grass," it seems to invite you to do just the opposite.

Becoming a Christian is a bit like when a new engine is put into a car. It would be foolish to simply admire the car and never drive it. But it would be equally foolish to push the car around with your own effort. Get in the car and drive, enjoying full use of the power the engine provides. Jesus is now living within you, and His power will strengthen you to live for Him.

Similarly, you are to "work out your own salvation." This shows that you have a massive part to play. But this verse continues, "it is God who works in you, both to will and to work for his good pleasure" (Philippians 2:12-13). So, change is the work of God, but we are not merely passive observers. We cooperate with the Holy Spirit who lives inside us.

WHAT DOES CHANGE LOOK LIKE?

The goal of change is to become more and more like Jesus. The more we love Jesus the more we will want to be like Him. We need Him to change our motivations. Jesus said, "If you love me, you will keep my commandments" (John 14:15).

Jesus' greatest commandment is to "Love the Lord your God with all your heart and with all your soul and with all your mind" (Matthew 22:37). This love will need to be developed over time, by Bible study, prayer, worship, and observing God's great faithfulness towards us.

Jesus tells us that the second commandment is, "You shall love your neighbor as yourself" (Matthew 22:39). We demonstrate our love for God by our love for others, even our enemies.

> Love is not a feeling, but a doing word.

Biblical love is very practical. Love is not a feeling, but a *doing* word. It is not an emotion, but an action. Jesus told us to treat others in the same way we would like to be treated (Matthew 7:12).

Paul describes love in 1 Corinthians 13. These words are worthy of much careful thought and prayer. Every decision we make should be based on what is the most loving thing to do. Allow God's Word to define what love is:

Love is patient and kind; love does not envy or boast; it is not arrogant or rude. It does not insist on its own way; it is not irritable or resentful; it does not rejoice at wrongdoing, but rejoices with the truth. Love bears all things, believes all things, hopes all things, endures all things. Love never ends. (1 Corinthians 13:4-8)

This is the core of how Jesus wants us all to live. If everyone loved like this, the world would be a very different place.

Change involves running away from sin. Jesus doesn't ask you to change so He can accept you. He already loves you and He is committed to helping you to change. Don't do the right things to impress Jesus, but rather do them because you love Him. He carries you, like being on an escalator, and moves you toward perfection. All this will only be fully achieved when we see Jesus face-to-face.

There are certain behaviors that the Bible warns us to flee from:

> Now the works of the flesh are evident: sexual immorality, impurity, sensuality, idolatry, sorcery, enmity, strife, jealousy, fits of anger, rivalries, dissensions, divisions, envy, drunkenness, orgies, and things like these. I warn you, as I warned you before, that those who do such things will not inherit the kingdom of God. (Galatians 5:19-21)

How can we stop doing such things? The first step is simply to decide that we are no longer going to live that way. There are radical decisions to make. For example, while Joseph was a slave in Egypt, his master's wife invited him to sleep with her. Joseph didn't play with temptation, but instead he literally ran away from her (Genesis 39).

Practical steps can be very helpful. For example, many recovering alcoholics find a new route to walk home to avoid the shop where they would previously have bought alcohol. Think carefully about what you can do to avoid the temptations that pull you away from following Jesus.

But even more important than exercising such wisdom is to cultivate the work of the Holy Spirit in us:

> The fruit of the Spirit is love, joy, peace, patience, kindness, goodness, faithfulness, gentleness, self-control; against such things there is no law. And those

who belong to Christ Jesus have crucified the flesh with its passions and desires. (Galatians 5:22-24)

Despite our sinful nature, there is something about these attributes that attracts everyone. Spend time thinking about what these things mean, and ask God to cause this fruit to grow in your life.

Jesus paints another beautiful picture of the Christian life in the Sermon on the Mount. He urges us to live in a way that turns the world's values upside down:

Blessed are the poor in spirit, for theirs is the kingdom of heaven.

Blessed are those who mourn, for they shall be comforted.

Blessed are the meek, for they shall inherit the earth.

Blessed are those who hunger and thirst for righteousness, for they shall be satisfied.

Blessed are the merciful, for they shall receive mercy.

Blessed are the pure in heart, for they shall see God.

Blessed are the peacemakers, for they shall be called sons of God.

Blessed are those who are persecuted for righteousness' sake, for theirs is the kingdom of heaven. (Matthew 5:3-10)

A major theme of these values is not to claim your own rights, but instead to prefer others to yourself. This comes from calming down and resolving not to give expression to every thought and impulse:

O LORD, my heart is not lifted up; my eyes are not raised too high; I do not occupy myself with things too great and too marvelous for me. But I have calmed and quieted my soul, like a weaned child with its mother; like a weaned child is my soul within me. (Psalm 131:1-2)

An important tactic in the battle against sin is to take control of your thoughts. Don't allow your mind to wander idly: "Take every thought captive to obey Christ" (2 Corinthians 10:4-5). You must not simply act on every brief impulse or emotion that passes through your brain.

It is vital to fill your mind with good things. If you put garbage into your mind, don't be surprised when garbage comes out:

The peace of God, which surpasses all understanding, will guard your hearts and your minds in Christ Jesus. Finally, brothers, whatever is true, whatever is honorable, whatever is just, whatever is pure, whatever is lovely, whatever is commendable, if there is any excellence, if there is anything worthy of praise, think about these things. (Philippians 4:7-8)

> An important tactic in the battle against sin is to take control of your thoughts.

At this point it is worth stating that for some people this battle is much more difficult than for others. Some Christians may be doing all the right things in terms of prayer, reading the Bible, and learning self-discipline. However, their thoughts become much more than fleeting, and the battle seems unwinnable. Even in our struggling, we are driven to depend on Christ more and to cry out for help. Often defeating specific sins may require the support and prayers of more mature Christians.

Sometimes struggling with negative or irrational thoughts can also be an indicator that it is time to reach out for professional help. Mental illness is very real, and it affects many people who cannot "pull themselves together." Their negative thoughts are too powerful for them to resist. They need multifaceted, holistic, and compassionate help, which should involve health professionals. Some people even despair of life itself. Be ready to encourage them to seek the help of doctors, and offer your support. Christians must seek to destroy the stigma and shame experienced by many who suffer in this way.

CHANGE REQUIRES THE HELP AND SUPPORT OF THE CHURCH
Change is not just a personal thing. It happens within the context of a supportive network of friends, which a good local church will be able to provide.

The Church is described in the Bible as a body, a family, and a building or temple for God. A solitary Christian disconnected from others cannot fulfil any of these models of the Church.

We need a church for many reasons:

1. **The Church teaches us the Bible.** Preachers, small group leaders, and Christian friends will share with you what they have learned. Be open to their wisdom, but test everything you hear with the Bible.

2. **The Church shows us how to live as a Christian.** You do not have to figure things out on your own. Get to know godly Christians, observe their lives, and ask how they have dealt with difficult decisions and their own struggles.

3. **The Church helps us see areas where we need to change.** We all have blind spots. A good Christian friend will always be a positive encouragement. But they may also

sometimes help you to see something you have missed. This is not supposed to be oppressive. Some Christians spend their lives unhelpfully pointing out every possible sin they see in the lives of others, and misery is the result. But if you trust someone who genuinely cares for you, and they are gentle with you, their advice can be invaluable.

4. **The Church is an environment for confession and repentance.** Over time, we hope you will be able to find a wise Christian friend who can lovingly help you back on track when you sin. We don't have to share our sins with everyone, but confessing to someone who is trustworthy often breaks sin's power.

5. **The Church provides an outlet for you to serve.** The Christian life is all about putting others first. Whether we simply make the teas and coffees at church, or do whatever else needs to be done, helping the community leads to great change in us.

God has a plan, promise, and purpose for your life. There is something He designed you to accomplish.

> For we are his workmanship, created in Christ Jesus for good works, which God prepared beforehand, that we should walk in them. (Ephesians 2:10)

He will weave you into what He intends you to become. He will do this in the context of serving a body of believers.

Most people wrestle with God and want to be like someone else. Quit fighting and accept what God has for you and be satisfied in it. Be yourself! But remember, God's purpose for you is tied up with fulfilling His purposes here on earth.

Make sure you are serving in your church, not only attending, but also being part of it. If you love God, you will find it a joy to serve in His house. If you care about His house, He will care for your house. Serve God gladly, and watch what He will do for you.

In summary, the Christian life is all about doing God's work, God's way, for God's glory. Christianity is a mobile faith; you are either moving closer to Jesus or further away. You are never static. Meeting Jesus changes you completely.

SEVEN PRACTICAL POINTS
FOR EFFECTIVE CHANGE

1. **Define reality.** If you are going to change, you must start with where you are. Some people foolishly try to pretend things are better already. They might say something like, "I am rich in Jesus' name," although they have no money in their bank account. Don't be unreal. Face the facts of your situation, however bad. Call a spade a spade, not an agricultural implement! God can help you no matter how bad your situation, but you must be honest about it.

2. **Take responsibility.** Don't blame other people for your mistakes or sins. Don't make excuses for your actions. Don't be like Adam, who blamed his wife, Eve, and even God (Genesis 3). If you are going to change, you are going to have to accept responsibility for your own mistakes.

3. **Define goals wisely.** Don't assume things. Assumption is the lowest form of knowledge. You need a clear goal. Be clear what Jesus wants to change, and plan how to go about it. In other words, ask what needs to be stopped, what needs to be started, and what needs to be sustained.

4. **Pursue diligently.** Discipline is the application of yourself to the task at hand. We have to persist, with resilience and determination, in our pursuit of a godly life.

5. **Reject passivity.** It is possible to be a success at work but a failure at home. The gospel helps us in every area of life. If we are passive, however, we miss out on its benefits. Reject passivity and laziness. Life passes passive people by. God wants you to be a pillar on which He can build, not an irresponsible lay-about.

6. **Assess the outcome positively.** Change comes in stages. Be patient. Learn to have a positive, faith-filled approach to situations, even when they are negative. Thank God for helping you make the progress that you do see.

7. **Approach change faithfully.** We are literally to be full of faith. We must cling on to hope even when change seems slow, or when we relapse. Keep praying, keep trusting God, keep believing. Ask others for help.

As we think practically about pursuing change we must never forget that the real key is in our connection to Jesus. As He said:

> Abide in me, and I in you. As the branch cannot bear fruit by itself, unless it abides in the vine, neither can you, unless you abide in me. I am the vine; you are the branches. Whoever abides in me and I in him, he it is that bears much fruit, for apart from me you can do nothing. (John 15:4-5)

QUESTIONS TO CONSIDER:

1. Are you determined to truly live for Jesus?

2. Have you grasped the wonder that God accepts you just as you are, but also wants to help you to change?

3. What is the first thing that you would like to see change in your life?

KEY BIBLE VERSES:

Luke 15:11-21
Galatians 5:19-24
John 15:1-17

6

Growing in your Faith: Reading the Bible

The best way to get closer to God, whether you have been a Christian for many years or you still have lots of questions, is to read the Bible. The Bible is the very words of God, and it contains everything you need to know about Him and how He wants you to live.

The Bible does not read like a modern novel. It is an ancient book, written during periods when those who could read would do so for hours, and even many who could not read memorized large portions they had heard recited. Television and the Internet were not around to impair their ability to concentrate.

The Bible will need to be read consistently and diligently if it is going to make a difference in your life. Someone who has not exercised for decades will not get fit by going to the gym only once, no matter how hard they work out. It is better to do a little exercise every day, and so it is with the Bible; read a portion every day.

Today, more than ever before, there are many Bible translations, books, software, apps, and Internet sites to help us understand God's Word. People often ask which translation of the Bible to use. The best version is the one that you will actually read. Choose a translation you can easily understand.

Bible versions range from those that aim to be more literal, to those that aim to be easier to understand. In English, the first group includes the King James Version (KJV) and the New American Standard Bible (NASB). The second group includes the Good News Bible (GNB) and the New Living Translation (NLT). A useful version that sits somewhere in the middle is the English Standard Version (ESV), which is the version we quote in this book.

If possible you should buy a paper Bible in which you can underline, make notes, and interact with the text. This helps you approach the Word of God in a reverent way, with the intent to focus on it, interact with it, and have an encounter with God speaking to you. An opened Bible demonstrates that you are taking God's Word seriously, not casually.

That said, many people also enjoy reading the Bible on a smartphone or tablet. However, make sure you enable "do not disturb" or "airplane mode" to avoid interruptions which would get in the way. It is vital to disconnect. We sometimes need to say, "Stop the world, I want to get off!"

WEBSITES TO HELP YOU STUDY THE BIBLE
http://www.esv.org
http://www.bible.com
http://www.biblegateway.com
http://biblia.com

Some people find that using an iPad or another tablet allows a greater focus on reading. This is because it feels more like reading a book than using a phone, which is so strongly associated with phone calls and text messaging, and so leads to distractions.

Several free Bible apps are available. Perhaps the most versatile has two names: "Bible" or "YouVersion." This contains translations in many languages and will read the Bible out loud to you. It can be used to follow a reading plan, such as the "ESV Study Plan," which covers the whole Bible in one year, including passages from several different parts of the Bible each day. Alternative apps include the "Bible Gateway" and the "ESV Bible," which has a clean look, and is also available as the "ESV Study Bible," including helpful explanatory notes.

Whether you are using a physical Bible or a mobile device, it is very helpful to write notes. Bible apps allow you to do this, but you may find a dedicated notebook will become something you treasure for years to come. Start collecting a list of favorite verses, categorized by subject, so you can easily find them in the future.

Get into a steady rhythm of life that includes a time for God's Word. Choose a quiet place in your home, and a quiet time of the day. Early mornings are often the best time to avoid distractions, and to prepare for the rest of the day. You need serenity and calm.

You may need to think creatively about how you can fit this time into your daily routine. For example, some hardcore commuters, who are very familiar with their journey into work, may be able to focus on reading the Bible on the train, or listen as they drive. Don't waste your commute.

WHAT SHOULD I READ?

The Bible is all about Jesus. Therefore, the best place to begin reading is often with one of the four Gospels, which record Jesus' life story: Matthew, Mark, Luke, and John. These are written from four different perspectives.

For centuries the Gospel that has stood out as most helpful for those who are not yet Christians is the Gospel of John. The writer says that he wrote it in order that we might believe. Jesus leaps off the pages and you are drawn to Him almost irresistibly. An old-time preacher used to dare his hearers to read this Gospel with an open mind, claiming they were almost certain to become a Christian as a result.

We recommend you get a good translation of the Gospel of John and read it this week. There are only twenty-one chapters so you could read three a day. Or, visit **hopereborn.com** and download a free guide to reading John's Gospel in forty days. Before you begin, ask God to speak to you. If you find yourself engrossed, keep going; you may find you read more than you had planned. Even if you have been a Christian for decades, we pray that as you read, a fresh love for Jesus will fill your heart.

When you have grasped the picture of Jesus that John paints, we would suggest you also read at least one of the other Gospels.

Matthew quotes passages from earlier books in the Bible that predict Jesus' coming and details of His life. He wrote with the Jews in mind. Because he includes a lot of Jesus' actual teachings, his book is often used to train new Christians.

Mark is the shortest and has an engaging style. If you want to read about the highlights of Jesus' life in a couple of hours, read the Gospel of Mark.

Luke was a medical doctor who carefully researched the facts in order to write an historical account. He does not assume you understand the rest of the Bible, and wrote for non-Jews.

Once you have understood the life of Jesus you could keep going and read about the Early Church in Acts which was also written by Luke. Most of the rest of the New Testament is letters, many of which were written by the Apostle Paul, and aim to explain the gospel. Or you could go back to the beginning of the Old Testament and learn how God prepared the way for Jesus' coming.

HOW SHOULD I READ?

Begin by reading large chunks to get an overview and understand the big picture. But the Bible is a very rich book, and individual phrases are likely to jump out at you. When this happens, write the verse down, and make sure you study the context so you do not misunderstand it. John Piper, a well-known pastor, once said, "Sentences change lives."

You may find it helpful to read portions of the Bible out loud since God promises blessings to those who do (Revelation 1:3). As you continue in your Bible reading we recommend you use the following widely used model. Routine is not enough. The technique is designed to help you get the most from your Bible reading, and connect with Jesus as you read. It has been described in various ways. You may find one of these mnemonics helps you remember the structure; they each refer to the same basic approach:

SOAP: Scripture, Observation, Application, Prayer

RAP: Read, Ask, Plan

FACT: Facts, Application, Confession, Thanksgiving

Practice the following steps as you read the Bible. Keep your notebook handy or Bible app open. Writing will help to make your thoughts clearer, and you will enjoy going back to your notes in the future.

Don't be overwhelmed with all the questions below; they are designed to get you thinking about what you read. You should not attempt to answer every single question, instead focus only on the ones that seem most relevant. If you don't know how to answer some of them, just leave them out for now. Later on you can always ask a wise friend, or read a Christian book that addresses the issue. To begin with, you can easily read a short passage and follow these steps in a few minutes. As you practice this, you will find that the longer you are able to devote to studying the Bible, the more you will benefit from it.

1. **Pray** about what you are about to read. Begin by worshipping Jesus, praising Him for who He is, and thanking Him for saving you. Ask Jesus to speak to you through what you read, and to help you to understand. You can use this prayer:

   > Open my eyes, that I may behold wondrous things out of your law. (Psalm 119:18)

2. **Read the Scripture.** Read at least a chapter, or perhaps a whole book if it is reasonably short. Then focus on a specific verse that seems important to you and read it several times.

3. **Observe the text, looking for the facts.** Don't rush into thinking about what this means for you today. Instead ask some of these questions.

   When and where did the events in this passage occur? Who was involved? What did they do? How did it happen? Why did things occur the way they did, and what were the outcomes? Who said what to whom? What would these verses have meant to their first readers? What do they mean in the context of the chapter they are found in, the rest of the book, and the rest of the Bible?

Our goal at this stage is to dig deeper into the text and understand it on its own terms. If you want to read other books to help you, make sure you have first spent some time thinking about the passage for yourself.

4. **Apply the text to your life and plan your response to it.** Often this requires us to discern the timeless principles of God's Word, and then apply them to the twenty-first century.

Ask yourself the question, "So what?" Is the message to you an instruction? Is it a fresh revelation of something you haven't previously understood? Is it an exhortation or encouragement? Is it a truth to declare? Is God correcting you and pointing out where your actions have not lined up with the Bible?

What is God saying to you through this verse? Listen for God's voice as you read.

Next, cultivate an action plan. Decide what you will do as a result of your reading. What will you change? Be careful not to take a phrase out of context and apply it in a way that would never have made sense to the first readers of the Bible. If you are uncertain of the implications for you today, discuss your thoughts with a more experienced Christian.

Be specific in your response to God's Word. What will be your first step? Why will you change? The answer should be because the Bible told you to change. Allow the Word to tenderize your heart. When will you change? Do it straight away, don't delay.

5. Pray about what you have read. Confess to God where you recognize that you need to change. Ask for Jesus' help to live in light of what you have learned. Thank Him for speaking to you through His Word, and for His unconditional acceptance.

WHAT SHOULD MY ATTITUDE BE TOWARD THE BIBLE?

Do not be casual in your approach to the Bible. It is not an ordinary book. It contains remarkable power that needs to be released to help you live the way Jesus wants you to. The Bible is awe-inspiring, "For the word of God is living and active, sharper than any two-edged sword" (Hebrews 4:12). God's Word is so powerful that it is the origin of everything:

> By faith we understand that the universe was created by the word of God, so that what is seen was not made out of things that are visible. (Hebrews 11:3)

The Bible's power is not released through merely reading. It's not enough to have the Word of God in your hand, or even to have memorized it, as helpful as those things are. The power lies in our believing it and approaching it reverently.

People who say they are Christians fall into various categories based largely on how they view God's Word. One group of people effectively treats the Bible with disrespect. They disagree with many of its teachings, and see it as mostly of historical interest. They set themselves above it, picking and choosing which bits to follow and which to discard when it does not match modern thinking.

They say things like, "I know that the Apostle Paul said that, but he was a man of his times, and things are different now; this is real life." Stay away from such people, and do not listen to them. Do not trample over the Bible, or tamper with

94

it. Jesus told us, "If you love me, you will keep my command-ments" (John 14:15).

A second group of people fails to pay attention to the way truth was gradually revealed over centuries as the Bible was written. Such people will often be very legalistic and promote harsh burdens that Jesus never intended us to carry. There are some things that the Old Testament says that the New Testament then supersedes. We must always interpret the Old in light of the New and not the other way around. For example, there were many laws about what the Jews should not eat. But God told the Apostle Peter that from now on He has declared all food clean (Acts 11:9).

There will always be things in the Bible that we will struggle to understand, and there are riches that we can spend the rest of our lives discovering. We should not get overly anxious about the parts we do not grasp, but allow God to speak to us every day.

As we read the Bible it seems clear that God intends us to interpret much of it literally. However, there are parts which use non-literal, poetic language, and can sometimes sound strange to our modern ears.

Certain parts of the Bible are difficult to interpret and apply. For example, four times the New Testament commands, "greet one another with a holy kiss" (e.g. Romans 16:16). Many Christians live in countries where friends would not routinely kiss each other. Most conclude that they can obey these verses by a friendly greeting, shaking hands, or hugging. Determining the principles that lie underneath instructions intended for an ancient culture, while ensuring we do not negate God's permanent commands, is not always straightforward.

Another group of people has almost the right approach to the Bible. They treat it with respect, and study it diligently, as the Bible directs:

> Do your best to present yourself to God as one approved, a worker who has no need to be ashamed, rightly handling the word of truth. (2 Timothy 2:15)

But we must not view the Bible simply as a textbook. It is possible to know a lot about the Bible but still fail to grasp its power.

Unfortunately some people set themselves up as experts in interpreting the Bible, and take great pleasure in stirring up arguments and division. Studying God's Word is helpful, but fighting about our differences with other believers never is.

Academic work, as helpful as it is, will never replace revelation. We must not read the Bible in order to simply become well educated. Mere head knowledge puffs us up, but if our knowledge of the Bible leads to real love for God, this builds us up (1 Corinthians 8:1).

We need the help of the Spirit to truly grasp God's Word, as "the letter kills, but the Spirit gives life" (2 Corinthians 3:6). We do not want to be like those who are "always learning and never able to arrive at a knowledge of the truth" (2 Timothy 3:7).

We must approach the Bible reverently. How we handle it reveals our attitude towards God Himself. He is not just your Savior; He is also your Lord. It is a privilege to listen to Him and bow in obedience. This is God's final message to the whole world.

We should long to meet Jesus, and worship Him as we find Him in the Bible. There is no substitute for true devotion and adoration. We need to cultivate a relationship with the Living Word, Jesus Himself (John 1:1-18). Time in the Bible is time spent with Him, and God rubs off on us:

> And we all, with unveiled face, beholding the glory of the Lord, are being transformed into the same image from one degree of glory to another. (2 Corinthians 3:18)

Sometimes our reading will seem mundane or even tedious, but we must keep going like a miner digging deep, looking for diamonds. Even in the middle of what can seem like obscure passages, we may suddenly see a glistening treasure which God has hidden for us. His Word suddenly comes alive to those who seek Him diligently. You might read the same words a thousand times, and then suddenly God speaks to you through them. Grasp hold of the eternal Word.

This view of the Bible leads us to focus on our daily time with faith, hunger, and expectation. When God opens your eyes to revelation, a single phrase can actually change the course of your life. Approaching God in this way is a holy moment.

The Bible is food for our souls. If we are hungry, it is not enough to go into a store and smell warm bread. Only a fool sniffs and leaves saying, "I've eaten." Just like food, you need to take in the Bible, chew it, digest it, absorb it, and allow it to nourish you, strengthen you, sustain you, and to rule over your life (see Jeremiah 15:16).

Just as we need to eat regularly to stay alive, we need to take in God's Word often. Jesus tells us, "Man shall not live by bread alone, but by every word that comes from the mouth of God" (Matthew 4:4).

Reading Christian books or listening to sermons, although helpful, are not the same as reading the Bible. Playing "Bible lottery" and simply choosing verses at random is not feasting on the Bible. Having an impressive theological conversation is not reading the Bible. We must hear God's voice for ourselves as we read. We need a relationship with the God of the Bible.

If you want God to listen to you, then your approach to the Bible will determine how He responds to you. God promises,

This is the one to whom I will look: he who is humble and contrite in spirit and trembles at my word. (Isaiah 66:2)

God is not looking for perfection in your life before He will care for you. He is not waiting for a deep academic understanding before He will reward you. He is expecting you to humble yourself before Him, and to respect His Word. There is much in the Bible to tremble about. It shows us how much we have failed to do what God wants from us. None of us have arrived. We need to acknowledge this before God, and ask Him to help us to live in the way He wants us to.

God wants us to "receive with meekness the implanted word" (James 1:21). If we ask Him to, He will take the words from the page and press them into us so that we truly change. Jesus promises, "You will know the truth, and the truth will set you free" (John 8:32).

When we see the Word of God as precious, we will want to memorize some verses, thinking about them over and over again. If you know how to worry, you already know how to meditate. Instead of anxiously turning over a situation in your mind again and again, fill your mind with a verse from the Bible so that it releases its benefits into your life.

Speak the Word out loud, and pray it back to God. Learn to speak it out. "I believed, and so I spoke" (2 Corinthians 4:13).

The Bible is Spirit-birthed and its actual words are life-giving:

The words that I have spoken to you are spirit and life. (John 6:63)

This does not mean we should act and pretend everything is fine if it plainly is not. Nor is it about money grabbing, as though claiming promises from God will make you rich. Don't despise the gospel, which offers much greater rewards than mere comfort in this life. When Jesus has spoken to you, align your thinking with what He has said. Pray and proclaim because you believe God's Word.

EXAMPLES OF BIBLE-BASED DECLARATIONS:

I am a child of God because I have accepted Him, and have believed in His name. (John 1:12)

I am forgiven, and my sin is covered. (Psalm 32:1)

I will not experience eternal death, but will have eternal life. (John 3:16)

God does not want to harm me, but has a hope and future for me. (Jeremiah 29:11)

God is at work for my good in every situation because I love Him and He has called me according to His purpose. (Romans 8:28)

He will supply all my needs according to His riches in glory. (Philippians 4:19)

I can do everything through His strength. (Philippians 4:13)

I will not be anxious about anything, but instead I present my requests to God. (Philippians 4:6)

God saved me by grace, through faith, and even that was a gift from Him. (Ephesians 2:8)

I will grow in love, joy, peace, patience, kindness, goodness, faithfulness, gentleness, self-control, because God's Spirit is at work in me. (Galatians 5:22-23)

Jesus has promised me life to the full. (John 10:10)

When I do sin, if I confess it to God, he will forgive me because He is faithful and just, and He will purify me. (1 John 1:9)

God has shown me how much He loves me: while I was still a sinner, Jesus died for me. (Romans 5:8)

When I am tired and weary, I will wait on God and He will renew my strength. (Isaiah 40:31)

Even in difficult times, Jesus is with me always. (Matthew 28:20)

Start your own list of verses that are important to you, and add to it over the years.

What are the benefits of reading the Bible?

Paul describes the Bible and what it accomplishes for us as follows:

> The sacred writings, which are able to make you wise for salvation through faith in Christ Jesus. All Scripture is breathed out by God and profitable for teaching, for reproof, for correction, and for training in righteousness, that the man of God may be complete, equipped for every good work. (2 Timothy 3:15-17)

If you want to be a true Christian, read the Bible. If you want to be taught by God, read the Bible. If you want to grow in your knowledge of God, read the Bible. If you want God to correct you, train you, and prepare you so that you can work for Him more effectively, read the Bible.

Basically, read the Bible.

Jesus Himself warns us that we must build our lives on His Word:

> Why do you call me "Lord, Lord," and not do what I tell you? Everyone who comes to me and hears my

words and does them, I will show you what he is like: he is like a man building a house, who dug deep and laid the foundation on the rock. And when a flood arose, the stream broke against that house and could not shake it, because it had been well built. But the one who hears and does not do them is like a man who built a house on the ground without a foundation. When the stream broke against it, immediately it fell, and the ruin of that house was great. (Luke 6:46-49)

Ultimately, our eternal destiny is at stake in how we choose to read and respond to the Bible. Saving faith is granted to us as we humbly read: "So faith comes from hearing, and hearing through the word of Christ" (Romans 10:17). Faith is a result of the work the Holy Spirit does in us, but He most often works through the specific word of God as we read the Bible, or its verses are quoted to us by others. This is why it is important for Christians to use the actual words of the Bible when sharing the gospel.

Reading God's Word and responding to it will give us power to resist sin. The way to stop sinning is to take His Word into our hearts:

How can a young man keep his way pure? By guarding it according to your word. With my whole heart I seek you; let me not wander from your commandments! I have stored up your word in my heart, that I might not sin against you. (Psalm 119:9-11)

God also promises peace to those who love His Word (Psalm 119:165), and who fix their mind on Him: "You keep him in perfect peace whose mind is stayed on you, because he trusts in you" (Isaiah 26:3).

If you believe God's Word, peace gradually begins to characterize your life. When you face challenges and anxiety begins to rise within you, calm down and go back to the Bible. Over time you will become a calm-spirited person. Even those Christians who struggle with depression or other psychological disorders, and may require medical help, often find that over time, Jesus fills them with a peace that others just can't understand.

The Bible grants us freedom and deliverance. Jesus promised, "If you abide in my word, you are truly my disciples, and you will know the truth, and the truth will set you free" (John 8:31-32).

God's Word will release great power in prayer. In an incredible promise, that sounds dangerous to our ears, Jesus says: "If you abide in me, and my words abide in you, ask whatever you wish, and it will be done for you" (John 15:7). Abiding in God's Word shapes our desires to line up with His. The Christian who is full of God's Word will not pray selfishly.

Studying the Bible gives wisdom for life. The psalmist writes, "The unfolding of your words gives light; it imparts understanding to the simple" (Psalm 119:130). Wisdom is found throughout the Bible, and one entire book, Proverbs, is devoted to teaching us practical principles to live by. Through the Bible, God shines His light on us and directs us so that we know which way to go: "Your word is a lamp to my feet and a light to my path" (Psalm 119:105).

The Bible is a mirror that reflects what we are really like, so we can stop fooling ourselves. We should use it wisely, and let it search us out, helping us understand where we need to change:

> But be doers of the word, and not hearers only, deceiving yourselves ... But the one who looks into the perfect law, the law of liberty, and perseveres, being no hearer who forgets but a doer who acts, he will be blessed in his doing. (James 1:22-25)

God's Word does us good in a more general sense. As we line up our lives with the Bible, God will bless us. He will prosper us, not necessarily in the sense of having more money to spend, but with the riches of true contentment, knowing life is lubricated by the peace and grace of God. God's promise to Joshua applies to us:

> This Book of the Law shall not depart from your mouth, but you shall meditate on it day and night, so that you may be careful to do according to all that is written in it. For then you will make your way prosperous, and then you will have good success. (Joshua 1:8)

God does want you to be successful and fruitful as a Christian. Reading the Word of God and meditating on it will help you achieve everything He has prepared for you to do. God has a plan for your life. He may not want you to be a high profile person, but He wants you to do well at what He calls you to be. Each of us has a different role that God has planned for us. None of us was an accident, and we are all equally important to God (see 1 Corinthians 12:12-26).

God's provision for you is released as you respond to His Word. If you choose to put Jesus first in your life, you will find that over time, many challenging situations will get resolved. Jesus is the expert in solving seemingly impossible problems. Some will seem to resolve themselves. Other situations will suddenly be unlocked by wisdom God unexpectedly gives you. However, you will often need to humbly ask for advice from others. Jesus will also sometimes change *you*, giving you a different perspective on an issue and the peace to live with what once seemed unbearable.

God's Word itself becomes precious to the believer, so that as we mature in God, we find that increasing happiness and contentment are to be found in reading its pages:

> Your words were found, and I ate them, and your words became to me a joy and the delight of my heart. (Jeremiah 15:16)

> How sweet are your words to my taste, sweeter than honey to my mouth! (Psalm 119:103)

God wants to make you a man or woman of His Word. There are many who think they are people of the Bible, but in reality they haven't even scratched the surface. The key is to continually submit ourselves to the Bible and allow it to change our hearts, as evidenced by a grace-filled and godly demeanor. As you read the Bible, God intends for you not only to be inspired, but also to be challenged and awakened.

Have you decided to follow Jesus? Then determine today that you will allow the Bible to dictate your whole life. Resolve to live in the Word even when you are not feeling any immediate benefits from reading it. Patiently persist, and wait for God to make it come alive to you.

Let the Word of God be so inside you that your thinking is affected and your speech is full of its values and phrases. Our use of the Bible in everyday conversation doesn't always have to be deep or even sound particularly spiritual.

For example, sometimes I (Adrian) find myself in conversation with work colleagues on the subject of how many people someone can realistically manage directly. I often point out, "Well, even Jesus only took on twelve, and actually one of them betrayed Him!" Every time I have used that biblical humor my colleagues have appeared intrigued. Usually the conversation has gone no further, but moments like that help others understand how important the Bible is to us, and how relevant it is.

Let every decision be guided by what you read in the Bible. Don't toy with it, but rather cherish it. Determine that every single day you will read this precious gift our Savior left for us.

CONCLUSION

The purpose of reading the Bible is this, to know God and to have encounters with Him on a daily basis, no matter how small.

As we close this chapter, we pray that the following words become a motto for your life and for every church:

> Let the word of Christ dwell in you richly, teaching and admonishing [or lovingly correcting] one another in all wisdom, singing psalms and hymns and spiritual songs, with thankfulness in your hearts to God. (Colossians 3:16)

QUESTIONS TO CONSIDER:

1. How have you approached the Bible up until now?

2. In light of what you have read, how will you change the way you approach reading it?

3. How do you plan to read the Bible? Where, when, and what will you read?

TO PRAY:

Ask God to make you a man or woman of His Word. Ask Him to reveal things to you as you read, and to shape you so that you become more and more like Jesus.

KEY BIBLE VERSES:

2 Timothy 3:14-17
John 8:27-36

7

Walking with Jesus: How to Pray

Prayer is simply communicating with God. Many Christians over-complicate this and find it difficult as a result. When you appreciate that God is your Father, and that He loves you, it will become natural for you to look forward to spending time with Him.

One of the secrets to a fulfilling prayer life is for your prayer to be entwined with the Scriptures. Always remember this: pray before you read the Bible, and pray based on what you have read.

Some Christians turn prayer into little more than worrying out loud. Presenting God with a long list of concerns, and asking Him to prevent bad things from happening is not what prayer is all about. Of course, we come to Him to ask for His help. However, first and foremost we are to worship and align our will with His.

There are different forms of prayer. You can pray short "help me" prayers as you go about your daily business. One of the best things to do as you prepare yourself for any task is to ask, "God, please give me wisdom to know what to do and say."

But, like reading God's Word, we do well to find a time during the day when we can devote ourselves to connecting with God. This can be during a time of Bible reading, or at a different time. Many people find that praying while out walking is very helpful. There is something about being surrounded by nature that can help us feel closer to the Creator.

You will probably find it more effective in the long run to make a habit of praying out loud when possible, although it may seem strange at first. Prayer is talking with God, so it is a good idea to actually speak.

We can best learn to pray by doing it with others. Praying with a mature Christian friend, a small group of friends, or the whole church can be inspiring.

Jesus' disciples saw how often He went out alone to a remote place to pray. Sometimes Jesus prayed very early in the morning. Other times He prayed all night. Clearly He took prayer very seriously. So His disciples asked Him to teach them how to pray. In reply, Jesus taught them this model prayer:

Pray then like this:
"Our Father in heaven,
hallowed be your name.
Your kingdom come,
your will be done,
on earth as it is in heaven.
Give us this day our daily bread,
and forgive us our debts,
as we also have forgiven our debtors.
And lead us not into temptation,
but deliver us from evil." (Matthew 6:9-13)

This is often called the Lord's Prayer, although we know that Jesus Himself certainly never prayed it as He never had to ask for forgiveness. It can be very helpful to work through the components of this prayer, using them as a guide as you pray in your own words.

RELATIONSHIP: *"OUR FATHER IN HEAVEN."*

Jesus' model prayer begins by reaffirming our relationship with God. He is not a heavenly headmaster to cower before. He is not a remote boss. He is a loving Father.

Just like in the story of the prodigal son (Luke 15:11-32), our Father will come running toward us whenever we come to Him, even if we don't feel His presence. Begin your prayer with who God is. Remind yourself that He loves you. He invites you into His presence despite your stained heart. Don't begin with confession or you may feel depressed and condemned.

Don't allow the fact that you may not have prayed for a long time to prevent you from coming to God. Come boldly into His presence, thankful for what He has done for you, and confident of the free access given to all who believe in Jesus.

> Let us then with confidence draw near to the throne of grace, that we may receive mercy and find grace to help in time of need. (Hebrews 4:16)

How wonderful that we have a loving and all-powerful Father who is always caring for us.

The word "our" is not insignificant. It indicates belonging, both to God, and to all our brothers and sisters in Christ. Together we are the family of God.

109

REVERENCE: *"HALLOWED BE YOUR NAME."*

Here we focus on the fact that God is in heaven, and His name is to be hallowed, or treated as holy. He is to be praised and worshipped. Linger in His presence often. Focus on His glory always. Remind yourself of all He has done for you daily. When you recognize how worthy He is and thank Him, it sets the tone for the rest of your prayer time. You could play some worship music and sing along to help you focus on Him.

RESPONSIBILITY: *"YOUR KINGDOM COME, YOUR WILL BE DONE, ON EARTH AS IT IS IN HEAVEN."*

This section is about requesting God's purposes to be fulfilled here and now. There is a day coming when this world will be filled with the glory of God, and when all pain and suffering will cease. In the meantime we ask, "Let this world reflect the world that is to come." We pray not just for our own comfort, but for the values of Jesus' kingdom to break into our homes, our churches, our workplaces, and the communities in which we live.

We may find ourselves mourning the latest tragedy that demonstrates how broken our world is. We appeal to God to rebuild families, comfort the suffering, and bring justice to the poor.

Like the disciples in Matthew 9:38 who are told to pray that God would send out workers into the harvest field, God will also ask us to be part of the answer to our own prayers. We are called to be kingdom agents to reach out to a dark world, as lights representing our Savior, Jesus, who is the Light of the world:

> You are the light of the world. A city set on a hill cannot be hidden. Nor do people light a lamp and put it under a basket, but on a stand, and it gives light

to all in the house. In the same way, let your light shine before others, so that they may see your good works and give glory to your Father who is in heaven. (Matthew 5:14-16)

We cannot pray, "Your kingdom come," without surrendering ourselves to His kingship and offering to play our part in extending His rule on earth. God is ultimately responsible for bringing this about, but He has a specific role and task for each of us in promoting His purposes.

REQUESTS: *"GIVE US THIS DAY OUR DAILY BREAD."*

We turn to reaffirming our reliance on God for everything. He has promised to supply all our needs "according to his riches in glory" (Philippians 4:19). He has more than enough resources to meet our needs. Like a humble child approaching his father, we ask God to provide for today, rather than worrying unnecessarily about the future.

God does not promise to make us rich. But He does promise to look after us. We also pray for God to meet the needs of others at this point, as an expression of our love for them.

It can be helpful to have a list of your requests and to keep a record of how God answers them, which will sometimes be in the most surprising ways. Don't expect God to always do things the way you think is best.

For example, you might pray that God would help you in your job, to remove the stress you are feeling because of a difficult boss. You would probably be very surprised if you lost your job the next day. The stress had been removed all right, but now you have no work. Imagine, however, your feeling if the following day you received a phone call from another company offering you a better job that you had previously applied for but had never received a response. God had abundantly answered, but for a day you might have been tempted to doubt His provision for you.

Not everybody's story will be that dramatic, and there may be times when it feels like God has forgotten you. Weeks, months, or even years might go by when your faith in His fatherly love for you is stretched to the limit. But remember, He is always caring for you, even during the hard times. And one day we will be with Him forever, and whatever trials we have experienced will be just a distant memory. God's plan may be different from ours, but it is always for our good:

> And we know that for those who love God all things work together for good. (Romans 8:28)

REPENTANCE: *"FORGIVE US OUR DEBTS."*

Having reminded ourselves that because of Jesus we have access to God in heaven irrespective of what we have done, having worshipped Him, and having spent some time requesting things of Him, we now turn to the confession of our sins, which Jesus refers to as debts.

This is late in the model prayer because God wants to remind you that He is your Father first.

No matter what you have done, if you are a believer, your sin has been covered and you are made righteous before Him. But we are to pursue a lifetime of repentance. We acknowledge the things that we have done that we should not have done, and things that we should have done that we have not.

This is not just about what we might think of as big sins, but includes acknowledging things like wrong attitudes, laziness, careless talk, or greed. Our sins are ultimately against

God, so we must turn to Him for forgiveness. You can read Psalm 51 for a model prayer of repentance.

Be specific. Ask God to prompt your conscience about sins you may not be aware of. Use the same words that the Bible does to describe sin, rather than polite euphemisms. As we pray, we realize that we are forgiven, feelings of guilt disappear, and we emerge with a fresh determination to serve Jesus.

RESTORATION: *"AS WE ALSO HAVE FORGIVEN OUR DEBTORS."*

Jesus is very clear that receiving forgiveness from God cannot be isolated from our need to forgive others. As you pray, you may be reminded of a broken relationship. If so, resolve to go and attempt to repair it. If you want forgiveness from God, you must be prepared to offer forgiveness toward others.

> If possible, so far as it depends on you, live peaceably with all. (Romans 12:18)

Thinking about ways to try to resolve difficult relationships is an area where you will benefit from the advice of a wise Christian. If you are struggling to forgive or be reconciled, find someone trustworthy to talk it over with. It is not gossip to discuss your problem with someone who can be part of the solution.

There may be times when you have genuinely done everything you can to resolve a difficult relationship. Forgiveness doesn't always lead to things being the same as they were beforehand. However, you must learn to let go of all bitterness, or it will consume you. When you hold on to hurts from the past, you harm yourself, not others. Forgiveness will bring release from any resentment that is slowly corroding your heart.

Ask yourself if there is anyone you need to forgive. Or perhaps you need to ask someone else for their forgiveness? Don't be unwise in this; you do not have to ask for forgiveness from someone every time you have a bad thought about them. Imagine the folly of saying something like, "Please forgive me, I have been constantly laughing at your singing voice in my mind every time I hear it in church." While you may well need to repent of this before God, your approach to the victim of your internal mockery, should be to simply look for a way to bless them, instead of telling them about it. There is nothing to gain by "confessing" such a sin to them. It may sound foolish, but some Christians think that doing so will make them feel better, and perhaps it does, but only at the expense of the person who had no idea that you had a problem with them in the first place.

We should not be naïve and unwise about what forgiveness means for our relationships with others. There can be times when a sin is so severe that it would be unwise to attempt to restore a relationship of trust too soon. Some sins are also against the law, and in such circumstances we will need to involve the appropriate authorities. This is especially true concerning abuse, when inaction could put others at risk. You can forgive someone but still report them to the police.

The critical question, however, is how seriously will you take Jesus' warning that He will not forgive you if you don't forgive others?

RESCUE: *"AND LEAD US NOT INTO TEMPTATION, BUT DELIVER US FROM EVIL.'*

We are fickle beings, prone to wander from our love for Jesus. There is also an enemy who would love to see us fall.

We should ask God to protect us from the schemes of Satan, and keep us from sin.

Of course, as we pray, we must also think of things that we can do to flee from temptation. There is no point in asking God to deliver you from a sin that you are playing games with. By all means pray that God will change your heart, but don't neglect simple yet radical steps that you can take to escape the clutches of sin. If, for example, you are tempted to watch things you know you shouldn't late at night on your TV, find a way to block those channels, or even get rid of cable TV altogether. Or if you find you argue with your husband or wife about the size of your credit card bill each month, cut your card up so that you can't use it any more.

Ultimately, sin hurts you, and you could end up destroying your family, your job, and your reputation for a few minutes of illicit pleasure. It really is not worth it.

The Bible shows us how to pray and what to pray. Look for verses that you can turn into prayers. The Psalms are full of examples, and include every emotion known to man, honestly expressed before God. They model to us that we should be open with Him, without being accusatory or disrespectful.

As an example, here are some excerpts from Psalm 25, which can easily be used in our prayers:

To you, O Lord, I lift up my soul...
let me not be put to shame ...
Make me to know your ways, O Lord;
teach me your paths.
Lead me in your truth and teach me ...
Remember your mercy, O Lord, and your steadfast love,
for they have been from of old.
Remember not the sins of my youth or my transgressions ...
For your name's sake, O Lord,

pardon my guilt, for it is great ...
Turn to me and be gracious to me ...
bring me out of my distresses...
Oh, guard my soul, and deliver me!

There are many other verses in the Bible that demonstrate what to pray. We encourage you to create your own list as you read.

Ultimately, we learn to pray by praying. The more you pray, the stronger your relationship with God will be, and the more encouragement you will have to keep on praying. Prayer will cause you to grow in your faith, and in your love for Jesus. Keep at it, even when it is difficult, and keep learning about prayer from other Christians who you respect.

CONCLUSION

As you finish reading this book, we pray that through its pages you will have become sure that you are a Christian, and grown in confidence to share the message of Jesus with others.

Living as a Christian frees us from guilt, and offers renewed hope and purpose. As you grow in your relationship with God He will draw close to you and provide for all your needs.

Press on toward the goal of knowing Jesus, both now and for eternity (Philippians 3:14). There is a glorious day coming when God will come and dwell with His people, there will be no more death, and He will wipe away every tear (Revelation 21:2-5).

May God keep you and protect you. May God Himself comfort you and encourage you. May you know God's presence. May you know the joy of sins forgiven. May God strengthen you and empower you to live as a Christian for the rest of your life.

We hope that you have found a good local church that will help and encourage you in your walk with God. Following Jesus is best done as part of a group of people who love and support each other. We pray that you will be blessed as you get to know your pastors and Christian friends.

No book can take the place of a mature Christian giving you practical advice and support as you learn to be a follower of Jesus. Just as aspiring business leaders will look for a good mentor, we would be wise to look for someone who will help us become a better disciple of Jesus. There is no solo growth in the Kingdom. Every Christian is born as a baby, and you need the regular nurturing that comes from wiser, more mature Christians who will disciple you in the way of the Lord and the Word of God. Discipleship is not optional, it is a natural next step for those who want to walk rightly with the Lord. We all have a part to play, both in allowing other people to teach us, and over time in teaching others.

Ultimately the Christian life is all about obeying Jesus' two Great Commandments: "Love the Lord your God with all your heart and with all your soul and with all your mind," and "love your neighbor as yourself" (Matthew 22:37-39).

We are also called to play our part in fulfilling the Great Commission, which was some of Jesus' last words to His disciples:

> All authority in heaven and on earth has been given to me. Go therefore and make disciples of all nations, baptizing them in the name of the Father and of the Son and of the Holy Spirit, teaching them to observe all that I have commanded you. And behold, I am with you always, to the end of the age. (Matthew 28:18-20)

About the Authors

Tope Koleoso is the lead pastor of Jubilee Church London, which is a multicultural church with over seventy nationalities represented across three sites in Enfield, Wood Green, and Ilford. He is also involved in planting and supporting other churches internationally, and is a Christian conference speaker.

Tope's sermons are available free online at:
jubileechurchlondon.org.

Adrian Warnock serves on Jubilee's leadership team, and runs a well-known Christian blog at **adrianwarnock.com.** He is also the author of *Raised With Christ – How The Resurrection Changes Everything,* published by Crossway. He is a medical doctor by training, and currently works in clinical research.

You can connect with the authors on Twitter:

@topekoleoso and **@adrianwarnock**

For free sermons about the subjects in this book, more information, or to purchase more copies of *Hope Reborn* please visit **hopereborn.com.** Free worksheets to help you apply the Bible study method described in Chapter 6 are also available. These include a forty-day guided reading plan for John's Gospel which is an ideal introduction to reading the Bible, or a refreshing approach if your Bible reading has become stale.

You can also connect on Twitter **@hoperebornbook** or on Facebook **hoperebornbook**.

Acknowledgments

We are both grateful to God for everyone whose sermons, books, and conversations helped to shape the ideas found in this book.

Many thanks to all those who have read drafts and suggested edits: Andrée Warnock, Andrew Fountain, Andrew Arulakshman, Anne Norrie, Annette Harrison, Chris Bennett, Charis Warnock, Chris Ebechidi, David Tingey, Donna Skaropoulou, Emily Priestley, Henry Warnock, Jo Soda, Joel Warnock, Kemi Koleoso, Liam Thatcher, Louise Legg, Lynn Ashworth, Mandy Johnson, Marco Tagliarini, Marjorie Warnock, Phil Butcher, Rice Broocks, and Tom Osborne.

We thank our families who support us in everything we do.

Most of all, we acknowledge our eternal debt to Jesus Christ who loved us before the foundation of the world, and who lived, died, and rose again to save us.

It really is all about Jesus.

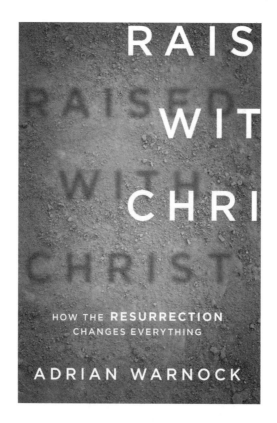

HOW THE **RESURRECTION**
CHANGES EVERYTHING

ADRIAN WARNOCK

ISBN 978-1-43350-716-8

Raised with Christ

ADRIAN WARNOCK

Jesus truly is alive today. But compared to his atoning death, Jesus' resurrection sparks relatively little discussion in the church. Inadvertently, we can become so focused on the good news that Christ died for our sins, that we almost forget he was "raised for our justification" (Romans 4:25). In *Raised with Christ*, Adrian Warnock exhorts Christians not to neglect the resurrection in their teaching and experience. Warnock takes his cue from Acts, where every recorded sermon focuses on Jesus' resurrection. He stresses that Christians who faithfully proclaim both the death and the bodily resurrection of Jesus, and live out the implications of that message in vibrant, grace-filled churches, will be enabled to reach a world that lives in death's dark shadow. The power of the risen Christ is active in every true Christian, transforming our lives. *Raised with Christ* will help you discover afresh the massive implications of the empty tomb. Jesus' resurrection really has changed everything.

Adrian is a first-rate communicator and a man whose life demonstrates the joy of Christ's resurrection. You will be greatly blessed by this book.

Albert Mohler

Finally, a new generation of readers has a clear and highly readable book on the resurrection of Jesus Christ.

Joni Eareckson Tada

With great clarity, Adrian teaches how the resurrection of Christ matters every day.

Ed Stetzer

FINALLY
ALIVE
JOHN PIPER

ɪsʙɴ 978-1-84550-421-2

Finally Alive

JOHN PIPER

When Jesus said to Nicodemus, "You must be born again", the devout and learned religious leader was unsure what Jesus meant. It would seem nothing has changed. Today "born again Christians" fill churches that are seen as ineffectual at best, and even characterized by the "mosaic" generation as "unchristian'.

The term "born again" has been devalued both in society and in the church. Those claiming to be "born again" live lives that are indistinguishable from those who don't; they sin the same, embrace injustice the same, covet the same, do almost everything the same.

Being "born again" is now defined by what people say they believe. The New Testament however defines Christians very differently.

> When Jesus said to Nicodemus, "You must be born again" (John 3:7), he was not sharing interesting and unimportant information. He was leading him to eternal life... If he does that for you (or if he already has), then you are (or you will be) truly, invincibly, finally alive.
>
> −JOHN PIPER

John Piper served as pastor of Bethlehem Baptist Church, Minneapolis, Minnesota for 33 years. He is the founder of desiringGod.org, a chancellor of Bethlehem College & Seminary, and he has written more than 50 books including *Desiring God* and *Don't Waste Your Life*. John and his wife Noel have four sons and one daughter.

MAGNIFICENT
OBSESSION
WHY JESUS *IS* GREAT
DAVID ROBERTSON

ISBN 978-1-78191-271-3

Magnificent Obsession

David Robertson

David Robertson, author of *The Dawkins Letters*, was told by the leader of an atheist society: "Okay, I admit that you have destroyed my atheism, but what do you believe?" His answer was "I believe in and because of Jesus." This book shows us why Jesus is the reason to believe. In response to the shout of "God is not Great" by the late Christopher Hitchens, David shows us why Jesus is God and is Great.

Engaging and insightful... This book is useful no matter what your experience and where you stand on matters of faith.

Tim Keller

Senior Pastor, Redeemer Presbyterian Church, New York City, New York

We will share this "Magnificent Obsession" so that ... friends may discover not only what it means but why it matters.

Alistair Begg

Senior Pastor, Parkside Church, Chagrin Falls, Ohio

David and I disagree on a great many things, but we are unified understanding the importance of this ongoing debate.

Gary McLelland

Atheist, blogger and secular campaigner, Edinburgh, Scotland

I love this book! It's an excellent, conversational introduction to Christianity for non-Christians and new Christians who are wrestling with questions.

Jon Bloom

President, Desiring God, Minneapolis, Minnesota

Christian Focus Publications

Our mission statement –

STAYING FAITHFUL
In dependence upon God we seek to impact the world through literature faithful to His infallible Word, the Bible. Our aim is to ensure that the Lord Jesus Christ is presented as the only hope to obtain forgiveness of sin, live a useful life and look forward to heaven with Him.

Our books are published in four imprints:

CHRISTIAN
FOCUS

Popular works including biographies, commentaries, basic doctrine and Christian living.

CHRISTIAN
HERITAGE

Books representing some of the best material from the rich heritage of the church.

MENTOR

Books written at a level suitable for Bible College and seminary students, pastors, and other serious readers. The imprint includes commentaries, doctrinal studies, examination of current issues and church history.

CF4•K

Children's books for quality Bible teaching and for all age groups: Sunday school curriculum, puzzle and activity books; personal and family devotional titles, biographies and inspirational stories – because you are never too young to know Jesus!

Christian Focus Publications Ltd,
Geanies House, Fearn, Ross-shire,
IV20 1TW, Scotland, United Kingdom.
www.christianfocus.com